Partnering Together

A Church Doing Mission in South Sudan

To Becky

from Craig

Craig Lindsey

Parson's Porch Books

Partnering Together: A Church Doing Mission in South Sudan
ISBN: Softcover 978-1-946478-00-9
Copyright © 2016 by Craig Lindsey

To order additional copies of this book, contact:

Parson's Porch Books
1-423-475-7308
www.parsonsporch.com

Parson's Porch Books is an imprint of Parson's Porch & Company (PP&C) in Cleveland, Tennessee. PP&C is an innovative company which supports people who live in poverty by allowing them to earn money by assisting in publishing books by noted authors, representing all genres. To help people in poverty, PP&C totally depends on the generosity of its authors and partners.

Partnering Together

Table of Contents

Part 5
Developing Mission 83

Introduction

This is a story of people acting in faith. At the time this story began, First Presbyterian Church, like most religious congregations in America, was struggling with identity, seeking to make a difference in the world. There were no plans or definitions at the US State Department, in Sudan, in the Presbyterian Church USA as a denomination, or in Skaneateles, NY for what needed to be done in South Sudan by whom, how, at what cost. All that was known, was that there were open questions. Except for a dozen years, civil war had been perpetuated from 1956 until 2016, in an extremely poverty-stricken, remote and undeveloped corner of the Sub-Saharan part of the South Sudan portion of East Africa between the two Nile Rivers. Not only was the population impoverished, and at risk due to isolation's lack of inoculations, they had no infrastructure for getting supplies, no roads to get there, there was not yet any legitimate government recognized with which to gain access to information or permission. Environmental conditions limited any access to six months each year; all knowledge of locations, resources, conditions and people, were anecdotal from child refugees who had escaped these circumstances in a time of trauma. The leadership of First Presbyterian Church had no agenda for involvement in this mission. We were asked to provide resources for sponsorship of refugees for a limited time, but that relationship of trust has become a partnership, a faith Calling.

Part 1

The Call to Mission

In the best circumstance, "mission" is the empowerment of one culture to grow in faith by putting their beliefs into practice, through assisting others to change their circumstance. In this way, mission is the identity of the Church. Mission is often mistaken for charitable acts of pity. To this author that difference is important, because charity has routinely been focused on the recipient, rather than why the donor is motivated. As "Charity" our sense of altruism for others can blind us to our own true motives. "Mission" recognizes the need of those giving to reach out, our need to give, cognizant of the effect on both, of assisting others. Therefore, "mission is a partnership," with both parties receiving something unavailable from any other. A significant problem in mission is how to assist and empower without being patronizing, paternalistic, dominant. Black Liberation Theologian, Jim Cone described that "White clergy addressing Black congregations, and Black preachers addressing White congregations are problematic; while Black leaders do preach to the Afro-American culture about poverty, there is need for Caucasian leaders to speak to White Suburban American culture advocating for "the other," because only in this way can change happen. (Union Theological Seminary: Systematic Theology, Sept 1981) This is the role for Straight, White Males in Christian Liberation Theology, other than as traditional Oppressors."

True symbiotic partnership is difficult, because circumstances are rarely equal, parity can only be found in trading for what both had been without, which may be an intangible, like the need to "do something" in faith, recalling that faith without works is dead. A covenant is a partnership. Literally the word "covenant" means "to cut into the flesh," a covenant creates a relational identity to be carved into persons. Life involves covenants of trust; as such, covenants evolve, change, deepen as each individual changes. When the individuals change the relationship of mission as a covenant partnership commitment, evolves, deepens, changes with every new circumstance involved, without end. "The Call" is not something static, or what a believer chooses, or decides to do. The Call is an intentional awareness of being part of something God is doing in the world. An enormous difficulty is how to partner in mission, because for centuries the Western World has been provider on its terms, and the 3rd World has been conditioned to receive.

One of the distinctions between poverty and affluence, between underdeveloped territories described as 3rd World and the over-consuming Western-world cultures, is access to choice. Access to choice is the very definition of "power". In poverty, the question is whether there is any meal today or not. There is no choice between chicken and beef, or morally wanting to be vegan, or whom you know who could get you a reservation at an exclusive restaurant. Access is power, in knowing from whom and how to receive what one desires. Poverty is a world where no one has choice. There is only the hope and prayer for survival to live another day. In affluence, the question is not only between choices, but having access to commit to additional unknown opportunities.

In June of 2001, members of The First Presbyterian Church of Skaneateles began a commitment to three refugees from Sudan, for three months. Exiting the airplane, the men were tall (6' – 6' 7"), gaunt, excited by the newness of everything, and exhausted, exhausted from days of travel from the Kakuma Refugee Camp in Kenya, to Brussels, Belgium, to New York City, to Syracuse, NY. As Africans, they had heard there would be something called "snow" in Upstate New York and they were unclear what snow might be, or even though it was June, when and how snow might arrive. Andrew Ruach was 6'0" and 118 lb., missing all twelve of his front teeth, on top and bottom between the incisors. Jacob Maggai Majok was 6'4" and 120 lb. with a ready

11

smile, a cherubic baby-face and the squint of someone with a bright inquisitive mind, poor vision, and personal life experience projecting a different reality. John Dau (Doe) stood 6'7", 125 lb.

John limped as he walked, and one eye did not track with the other. Being refugees, each were assigned the birth date of January 1ˢᵗ, though John was roughly 27 years of age, Jacob 24 and Andrew 23 years old. They had each been at Kakuma Refugee Camp for 9 years, and a Refugee Camp in Ethiopia for 8 years prior, so John had been about 10 years of age when war struck his village, Andrew and Jacob had been children of 6 and 7, all were cousins.

These refugees came from a part of the world without electricity, technology, or plumbing. Ladies from the church demonstrated with all the patience of mothers, how to use a toilet, sink, shower, a telephone and television, how to cook and clean for themselves. Prior to the war, the Dinka tribe had lived in tukuls, round huts 10 feet in diameter, made of sticks plastered with mud, with a thatched roof. In this tukul, an entire family of two adults and 2 to 12 children would cook, eat, play and sleep. They knew not of beds or chairs or tables, separate rooms, of privacy, of bathing or a toilet; knew not of schools, reading, writing or mathematics; knew not of business, or economies, or storage. For thousands of years, the tribe had existed without concern for the future. What was important was family learning from one another. When war came, families were lost. In refugee camps family-identities were formed when older boys took care of younger ones as if still within a tribe but without parental adults. Coming to America, whole new possibilities opened, but at the cost of being further cut off from all those who had provided identity: extended family, parents, tribe, age mates, mentors and culture.

Divine Intervention

One of the first "divine interventions," was that rather than any one individual, or family, or the church as an institution, claiming responsibility for these young men as "sponsor," instead a clipboard was passed throughout the congregation on Sundays during worship. Each individual/ every family was encouraged to volunteer, to respond to the Call, to make a specific sacrifice of a day. On a given Sunday, on your day, to drive the 32 miles to the northeast side of Syracuse, where the men lived in an apartment complex with other Sudanese refugees, then return 32 miles southwest to Skaneateles, to attend worship at 9:30am; after worship to go to lunch together or bring the men to their homes, to share the afternoon as family, and at the end of the day to drive them back to Syracuse and return. This was a commitment of one Sunday, gas for 128 miles, and vulnerability to allow these strangers to enter your life for a day. Describing this as "A Calling" seemed overly dramatic, yet this is the way conversion of faith takes place. Not through the clouds parting and the Hand of God touching you, but signing a clipboard with your name to help someone in need by volunteering to share your day, on the Lord's day. In this way, John, Jacob and Andrew would learn how American families relate and function, how to shop in a grocery store and cook for themselves, as well as the names and relationships of every person in the Church. This filled their void for family and culture and mentors, by the Church learning the importance of their own relationships and identities. While this was never an intentional program decision, no decision has more positively affected this Church, than passing a clipboard for each person to accept their Calling to serve as partners in mission.

An Intentional Choice

However, while the church had a personal and faith commitment to these men, they, like all creatures were independent with a freedom of human will. The boundary was that the church could partner with the men, but could not dictate how they should live. The US State Department had explicitly stated that, as sponsors, the church could not proselytize these men, because the relationship of sponsor would be a power position that would not allow refugees to choose with freedom. Ironically, being a Mainline Protestant congregation in the Northeast United States, First Presbyterian Church hardly knew what "proselytizing" meant, but interpreted that the church would not/could not encourage church membership. However, another congregation did begin actively recruiting and evangelizing these Sudanese refugees to be members, and the First Presbyterian Church chose to trust them as adults, saying nothing. After several months, the men described, that other sponsors had challenged and ridiculed their friends who were refugees for "going astray." By allowing them to make their own choices, John, Jacob and Andrew, had been free to choose to act as equal partners with the leaders of First Presbyterian Church. This decision, to be free to choose, would come back again and again, as church leaders weighed whether to direct choices, or support the Sudanese in self-sustaining their own development.

Over a first meal together in their new apartment, the young men were filled with questions, most pressing of which, were three:

1) Out of 18,000 Dinka refugees at Kakuma, with 2,000,000 killed and 5,000,000 displaced, why were we chosen to save?

2) You have given us so many things we never had, we never knew existed. But where are our Bibles?

3) "Why did America not come to our rescue over twenty years? Why did you not care?"

Refugees of Civil War

The church had forgotten that they needed to have Bibles, and had been naïve about salvation, because the church's previous experiences of relocating refugees had been with middle-income, adult families from war-ravaged parts of Europe (Amsterdam and Rotterdam in 1945), (Croatia in 1997), and Southeast Asia (Viet Nam in 1976); and North American Mainline Christianity had become a programmatic faith based on consumerism.

These refugees had been first generation Christians, escaping civil war that in addition to race, military, natural resources and economic profit, was motivated by religious condemnation. The refugees had also been children, who after seeing their villages destroyed had personally walked, step-by-step for 1,000 miles across sub-Saharan Africa to find refuge. While refugees from Sudan living in Ethiopia, the Ethiopian government had also been overthrown, and these child refugees were then marched at gunpoint to the river. Like Hebrew slaves, these escaping refugees were pushed by the military to choose between death from technological weapons, or death in the water. On the other side of the river, the children could hear the gunfire of war in their home of Sudan, in the river before them were crocodiles and snakes, but behind them Ethiopian soldiers forced the children into the river firing over their heads and vowing to shoot them if they did not leave Ethiopia. Being chased in the river by crocodiles, swimming from one war zone back into another, all while children around them drowned and were killed by beasts they prayed to God to be saved. Their thoughts were of salvation from death, salvation from the life they knew, salvation from the horrors they were living. These Christians believed the only force that kept them alive and held back the chaos was Almighty God. The Bible was more precious than life itself, and salvation was not a warm feeling or a cathartic moment, not a decent and ordered committee structure, salvation was a life and death trust in God. Sunday morning, the pastor presented each in turn with his own Bible, and the refugees described, "Pastor, the deacons did their work very well. They each extended the ministry and peace of Jesus Christ to us."

In the weeks that followed, John had surgery for removal of a bullet and damage to his left leg. John also had corrective surgery for nerve damage to his eye that had been sustained in the war. Andrew was fitted for surgically implanted front teeth. Jacob was diagnosed as being near-sighted with astigmatisms and was fit for glasses. Many thought, how frightening, to come to a strange culture, thousands of miles from all you have known, and immediately to endure surgeries! However, it was during this time, before they were eligible for school or work that American Health Care was available to them for free, and an idea was planted of what could be.

Genocide Upon Genocide

Later, the church was to learn that this war in Southern Sudan began in 1983. Ethnically, the people of South Sudan are of several tribes (Dinka, Murle,

Nuer, Lou Nuer), the largest of which being the Dinka. While never linked in the Bible, 19th Century Western European Missionaries and indigenous preachers interpreting their own experience, cast the South Sudanese as a punished sinful people, identified with the Biblical people of Cush. The Cushites were a people of Genesis, identified as punished by God. Cush had been a son of Noah, who brought shame on his ancestor by seeing his father drunk and naked; later the Cushites were also descendants of those who did not listen to the prophet Isaiah, none of which could be proven or was accepted in Orthodox Christian teaching. The Capital of South Sudan having been Bor, and the ancestral center of the Dinka Tribe being the region of Duk. When the British eventually abandoned policies of Colonialism in the late 1950s, the British Empire had demarcated all Sudan as being one nation, whose land surface was equivalent to three times the landmass of the US State of Texas. Within that Nation were to be two peoples, ruling and serf, principally Arab in the North and African in the South. In addition to the anticipated racial, religious, cultural differences there were differences of language (language being the primary difference between tribes).

The North of Sudan was heavily industrialized, educated, trained in commerce, travel and western government. The South of Sudan was described as a wilderness, filled with harsh desert and natural resources, sub-Saharan savannah, volcanoes, outcroppings of forest. The biological composition of the earth of the South was extremely fertile, being the flood plains of the Blue and White Nile Rivers. Here Antelope, Wildebeest, Elephants, Zebras, Lions, Leopards and Hyenas migrated across the land in peace and co-existence, as nature had been since Eve and Adam left the convergence of the Tigris, Euphrates, and Nile Rivers (the Garden of Eden). In religion, the North had been predominantly Muslim; while the South prior to 1972 had been predominantly "Animist" attending to ritual blood/ animal sacrifices at the instruction of Tribal Witch Doctors. Throughout the 1800s, Missionaries from the Presbyterian, Anglican and Catholic Churches had planted seeds to evangelize Sudan for Christ; yet the primary instigating event for conversion had been oppression by the Muslim North, resultant in the South converting (1972-1983) as first-generation Christians.

Due to these stark differences and power advantages for the North, the first genocide had been cultural and educational. The only schools anywhere in Sudan were boarding schools in the North, where Arabic was spoken exclusively, and Islam was a required curriculum. In this way, like the Biblical Book of Daniel, the schools attempted to separate the children from their culture, encouraging them to adapt through education to live in the populated culture of the North.

The second genocide had been for "progress" and economic expansion. To aid trade and commerce, the Egyptian and French Governments united with the Government of Sudan to dredge a canal 20 feet deep 100 feet wide and over 300 miles long, to eliminate days of transportation as the White Nile cuts west at Juba, on the river's journey northward, before returning east at Malakal. If successful, this Jonglei Canal System would have reduced the journey for cargo by over 200 miles. However, the undertaking ignored the realities that indigenous villages had occupied this region for as long as records could describe, and herds of animals crossed this region on their seasonal migrations. 100-foot-wide 20-foot-deep canals suddenly dredged where none had been previously, flooded whole villages, and created an obstacle drowning millions of animals.

When Jonglei Canal construction was stopped because of fighting, the workers burned their bulldozers, trucks and cranes, to create barriers to future development. When Chevron Corporation discovered significant reservoirs of oil in the South, Northern Sudan government efforts shifted from ignoring the existence of an indigenous population to their extermination.

The battle was to have been a swift, decisive "extermination," as the Northern military possessed trucks, mortars, artillery, machine guns, while the Southern "militia" were stone-aged tribal cattle herdsmen, possessing little more than spear, bow and arrow, and machete. However, the Southern warriors were numerous and were fighting for their land and villages; where the Northern military were largely Darfur Jinjaweed mercenaries paid to kill infidel non-Muslims. In addition to knowing the local terrain, and having vastly different incentives, the Southern people were hunters and gatherers, accustomed to finding and repairing cast-off, broken materials, which in this case became weapons and vehicles.

As described by Martin Deng Leek, the decisive battle came when the Northern Sudan army trapped the Southern Sudanese militia (called the SPLA, Sudan Peoples' Liberation Army) against the border of the Democratic Republic of Congo. The SPLA were outnumbered and out-weaponed, without ammunition, they had witnessed the burning of their families, their homes and villages. It had rained for eighteen weeks, causing the vehicles of the Northern army to move slowly over swampy terrain, and emotional spirits to be dark. The SPLA knew they would all be killed in the next attack, together they passed word of the Biblical story of Joshua at Jericho, praying, then they rose with the fierce conviction of a man in torment. They screamed and attacked, rather than waiting to be destroyed. Miraculously, the invaders, demoralized by the rain, the mud, the lack of food, and suddenly terrified, fled. They abandoned trucks and barrels of diesel, armored vehicles, artillery, weapons, ammunition, food and fresh water. Simultaneously, the United States in retaliation for 9/11 had begun attacking Afghanistan and Iraq, declaring these and Sudan to be part of an "Axis of Evil in the World". While an unintended outcome, the United States demonstrating a willingness to attack Muslim nations, forced the Khartoum Government of Sudan to an accountability at the bargaining table for peace with Southern Sudan.

The Peace Plan that was forged was that for seven years (2005-2011) North and South would dwell as one nation, with the President of South Sudan functioning as Vice President of North Sudan, and vice versa. John Garang, leader of the SPLA and President of Southern Sudan was to be the embodiment of Peace in his own life. In January 2011, there would be a Referendum vote of the people, whether to allow Southern Sudan to secede to form a separate nation. Tragically, within a year after the Peace Plan had begun, John Garang was killed in a helicopter crash.

Over twenty years, villages had been burned, women raped, men, women and children enslaved and sold as human chattel. Extermination practices had included the forced sterilization of captured men and boys, by piercing their testicles with a needle or a nail; teaching the people that the soil in the South was so contaminated that any produce grown there would be poisoned; using the humanitarian crisis of sexually transmitted disease (particularly HIV), to teach the fallacy that one means of eliminating disease would be for an infected man to force sexual intercourse upon a virginal girl, the end result of which was instead to further spread the disease upon a next generation by abuse.

Twenty-seven thousand children fled their villages, after watching their homes, villages and families burned, then walked across the country to refuge in Ethiopia. In groups of two, three and five, they hid in trees and underbrush, they lay in swamps covered in water, being bitten by mosquitoes, while breathing through reeds. They sucked moisture from out of mud. They drank urine from humans and animals; ate any decaying scrap they could find. All the while, they were stalked by predators, lions, leopards, hyenas, carrion, and by soldiers. Any children captured that were not killed, were en-scripted into the Lords Resistance Army as child soldiers. These children believing they could not die, were given machete knives and brainwashed to attack their own people as enemy.

The third question that was asked by the three refugees that first night in America was "Why did America not come to our rescue over twenty years? Did you not care?" In truth, the people of America did not know and had not cared. Throughout the 1980s and 90s, America had been preoccupied with Iran and the Holy Lands, with drug wars in Latin America, with the dismantling of the Soviet Union, with sexual abuse in politics. America had avoided knowing about Rwanda, Ethiopia, Uganda, Congo and Sudan, as if ancient tribal wars that could never be solved, and were not the business of the United States or other parts of the Developed 1st World.

September 11, 2001

A fourth Sudanese refugee, Santino Atak, was due to arrive in America for sponsorship by the First Presbyterian Church on September 11, 2001, coincident with the conclusion of the original three-month sponsorship of John, Jacob and Andrew. Instead of arriving, the plane from Africa along with all other planes to the United States that morning, were returned to their place of origin.

On that evening, Tuesday, September 11, 2001, the people of Skaneateles, New York, gathered at the First Presbyterian Church. Rev. Craig Lindsey had gathered the Catholic and Protestant clergy to share in prayer. The pastor, spent the entire day in grief counseling and prayer services at local factories and corporate business headquarters. He preached that evening on the passage Jeremiah 4: 23-28.

> *I looked on the earth, and lo, it was waste and void;*
> *and to the heavens and they had no light.*
> *I looked on the mountains, and lo, they were quaking, and all the*
> *hills moved to and fro.*
> *I looked, and lo, there was no man, and all the birds of the air had*
> *fled.*
> *I looked, and lo, the fruitful land was a desert, and all its cities were*
> *laid in ruins*
> *before the Lord, before his fierce anger.*
> *For thus says the Lord, "The whole land shall be a desolation;*
> *YET I will not make a full end.*
> *For this the earth shall mourn, and the heavens above be black, for I*
> *have spoken,*
> *I have purposed; I have not relented; nor will I turn back.*

Lindsey professed, that they had read the very same passage only two days before, in every Catholic and Protestant pulpit in town and across the country, but now, to all, this Word had different meaning. This had not been the work of God, as Jeremiah envisioned, but, like turning the Genesis' story of the Creation of life backwards, the description was painfully appropriate. The preacher described the effects of human inhumanity to one another in war, and how everyone and everything, even creation itself, is destroyed. The most insidious nature of this verse and the current reality, said the preacher, is the absolute deafening silence, as reports were that they could find no sign of life, no voices, no birds, everything at Ground Zero was scorched and burned and crushed to ash, in what had been the most populated thriving part of our busiest metropolis; the heat rising from the ground causing everything to move to and fro; the crushing of the buildings so traumatic to the foundations, that the earth continued to quake in aftershocks.

The preacher described that in the congregation that night were refugees from civil war in Sudan who had recently come here to avoid this kind of destruction. We had thought America was insulated and secure for refugees, yet the reality of human hate is that nowhere is safe. But rather than being filled with fear of airplanes being used to crash into buildings, rather than hate against the persons who had done this, the only way to make real and lasting change was to reach out to all those in need and create new homes and new places for life together. The refugees responded by describing, "This bombing, therefore we sought to leave our home and come to America, those are not a people to be trusted." The pastor patiently and sternly said "No. People are people. This only demonstrates that people can be capable of atrocious acts, even to reversing God's creation, for humanity to make the world into a waste and void. But as children of God, we have to find ways to create trust and hope."

John Dau's Plan for Family Re-Unification

The next several months, the Sudanese refugees worked at jobs, trying to acculturate to become part of this new country. In December, Santino did arrive, and joined Jacob, Andrew and John. Throughout these first years in their new country, each of the Sudanese refugees tried to find and contact family members who had survived the fighting. In addition to personal desire for family, what could be a greater act of defiance and civil disobedience against genocide of a people, than personally re-unifying those dispersed by war! As refugees moved from camp to camp and to other countries, they shared information of who they knew and where family might be located. John Dau's efforts were complicated because while in America his name was spelled DAU, the meaning was only as "John Doe." However, one Sunday morning in 2003, John came walking up to the church, literally grinning from ear to ear and dancing. John announced, "Pastor, the Bible says, "The dead have come back to life, the lost have been found." I have proof that those words are true! I spoke with my brother, then with my mother whom I knew to be dead, and they are alive in Uganda!" John described that after speaking with his brother, they gave the telephone receiver to his mother. John's mother said, "You cannot be my son, John died at eleven years old. You, you are a man." She then hung up the phone. John called back, and explained that twenty years had passed, and he had now grown into a man, standing six foot eight inches in height.

Over the next year, John learned that one sister had had a difficult pregnancy and nearly died. She needed surgery. Could the church accept the calling of being responsible for the extended family of this refugee, providing her health care? The church stepped up to raise funds to help. Simultaneously, John worked to have his parents immigrate to the United States, but this was complicated because Dinka culture is a polygamous culture and John's father had several wives. If John's father Daniel Deng Leek should come to America, he would be abandoning his other wives, or committing bigamy. John's mother Anon Leek and John's younger sister, Akuot, who was born after the family had separated, did immigrate to Syracuse with the church co-sponsoring John's sponsorship of them. When his mother and sister came down the gangway at the airport, the reporters began flashing photos, and Anon collapsed to the floor holding John and weeping.

On Sunday morning, John and his sister and their mother Anon, all came to worship at the Presbyterian Church. During the Assurance of Pardon, Rev. Lindsey invited John and his mother to come forward to the Communion Table to introduce her. As she walked, Anon took three steps forward then rocked back a step, as if on a religious pilgrimage Anon sang a hymn of thanksgiving as she walked, interspersed with a high pitched falsetto guttural scream, "YaYayayayayayayayayayaya". Impressed by the emotion and faith of this, Rev. Lindsey asked the meaning of this scream, and as patiently as explaining the obvious to a fool, the pastor was told "This is the Angels' sound of Alleluia!"

The pastor named that "In the Gospel of John, there is description of Jesus' crucifixion. During which, two persons, the beloved disciple, John and Jesus' mother, standing at the foot of the cross. Jesus proclaimed "Mother, behold your Son. John, behold your Mother." Surely this day, these words had been fulfilled anew." Upstate New York Presbyterians tend to be known for stoicism as "the frozen chosen", rather than having testimonials and charismatic worship. That day, this congregation came to life with the Holy Spirit.

In these years, together, the church had reclaimed identity in the neighborhood as a community center and resource, as a venue for music and the arts. Great efforts had been made to name and work through existing circumstances of conflict. But for "resurrection of faith" to truly occur the congregation needed to wrestle with their commitments, with whether mission is only a program of charitable giving and sponsorship of others, or whether the church could risk to act with fresh energy, inclusion, intelligence, imagination and love. Risking even at danger to one's own safety and security and possessions and existent faith. This was a risk of challenging the church's accepted traditional aristocracy and bureaucracy, for new life to begin again as an adolescent, making mistakes, but trying to grow into new covenant partnerships.

In the process, this church also created a new paradigm for how to do mission. While projects like sponsorship of refugees might be accountable to the Session through the Mission Committee, and all administrative and program costs paid by the church for the first several years, once established, mission projects could develop their own Board of Directors, corporate status and Federal Tax Identification as independent non-profit 501c3 corporations. In this way, mission work which the church is invested in and wants to see succeed, grows beyond the church, with the church giving up all control.

Part 2

Developing Relationships: Finding the Lost Boys' Home

In August 2004 John Dau and a Sudanese named Paul Ariik participated in a United States gathering of Lost Boys at Salt Lake City, Utah. Here the Sudanese Refugees discussed how they might organize and serve their villages and families. November 2004, John Dau, Jacob Majok and Paul Ariik came to the Session of The First Presbyterian Church, describing that the long Civil War finally was drawing to conclusion. The Session waited for them to describe plans to return home to Sudan. Instead, they named that they could do more for their families and community here in the United Stated than they could by returning to Sudan now. In addition, they did not yet have American Citizenship to be able to visit Sudan; if they did enter Africa, they would not be allowed to leave again. Then they unveiled their dream. "We have been blessed here with resources that people in Southern Sudan have never known. In Sudan, there are no roads connecting places, so people travel by foot. The nearest medical doctor is over 70 miles away. When people become ill, someone else must carry them, or they die. We would like to build a Clinic in our Village, and we would like you to share in this with us. We have never built something like this, so we need advisors, architects, builders, doctors and people willing to help."

American Care for Sudan Foundation

Thus began, The American Care for Sudan Foundation (ACSF), later to be re-incorporated as The John Dau Foundation, a 501c3 Not for Profit, Faith-based Corporation, extending the ministry of the Church beyond a normal mission to raise funds and do mission internationally. Originally (2004), ACSF included Jack Howard, an 80 year old retired chemical engineer, who served as foster grandfather to John Dau; Richard Way who owned and operated several stone quarries; John Ayer, a retired Medical doctor who decades before had done limited mission work in developing countries; Steve Meyer, an Officer of the Welch/Allyn company; Ginny Stehle, who worked in distribution of discontinued products and marketing at Welch/Allyn durable medical equipment company; Susan Meyer, of the Presbyterian Church Mission Committee; Jack Capron, who was both a CPA and Attorney; Bill Stevens, a Project Manager with Niagara Mohawk Utilities and a general contractor; Connie Brace, a Syracuse Architect; Jim Vedder, a retired professor of Business Management who had done US/AID investigations; Peggy Surdam the Church's Business Administrator Treasurer, and the pastor Rev. Craig Lindsey; all of whom were part of The First Presbyterian Church. Their goal had been to raise $30,000 John Dau's estimated costs of materials and shipping of the Clinic, but the critical question was how to begin. The Dinka had no education, no comprehension of building techniques; even of "the wheel" was among the most rudimentary of developments they had been isolated from. The Sudanese in America had not been to South Sudan since they were children. Not only would perceptions be different, but decades of war would have changed topography and resources. At this moment, while pledged, the war had not yet ended; transportation, access, authority, ownership of land were unanswered questions and there was no communication.

ACSF began with basic questions, why build a building at all? The Dinka are a nomadic tribal people, so why build a building in a location? Given the war, would a hospital building with a large cross on the roof be a target for attacks? If any building were created, where should it be, and who should decide? Could land be purchased and owned? How do you hire contractors, when the population do not know construction techniques, and they trade in cattle rather than a hired wage? What building materials would be needed and what was available? Given that the population had survived in refugee camps for decades, could they be encouraged to pay for medical services, and if so in what currency, and how? Would the people help in building, did they have any skills, or would ACSF need to hire and import contractors? Each question seemed to lead to more questions and no specific objective answers.

Valentines' Day weekend, on February 13, 2005 "The First Presbyterian Church's Clinic Task Force", as it was called in the earliest days, invited David Bowman to share his experience. Bowman was a dentist from Grand Rapids, Michigan, who was involved in building a hospital for the Southern Sudanese at the Village of Waw. He described having dedicated his life to working at this for five years, and still, not yet having anything on the ground in Africa.

David Bowman offered the following guidance, from his experience:

> **Lesson 1:** "TIA: This Is Africa". Everything takes time; every relationship involves some level of corruption and subterfuge. In America, we are accustomed to time being money and to contracting; in Africa, the currency is cattle, and time is measured in generations not days or weeks or even years.

> **Lesson 2:** "Someone has to develop trust". In America, everything begins with contracts, legal documents, memos of understanding, budgets and calendars. North America is based on time and money and access to choices that allow priorities to be chosen. In Africa, nothing begins until someone goes to meet the leadership face to face, and after talking together, worshiping God together, sharing a meal and gifts, there is a partnership of trust established for a future to be forged. A relationship of trust is a commitment, a covenant that lasts generations, a Calling. From this basic trust, money, time,

commitments all flow naturally. Without trust, everything is a decision, weighed on its own merits, compared to other choices.

Lesson 3: "Tech Serve, Inc." is a Mission based corporation out of Green Brier, Arkansas, USA, which specializes in prefabricating elements of buildings, loading these into shipping containers for on-site erection in developing countries where materials are scarce.

Finding the Lost Boys

The next "divine intervention", or as it came to be described "evidence of God's humor", came in response to Rev. Lindsey's experience as pastor at the Skaneateles Presbyterian Church. The Church had previously been divided by a failed co-pastorate, decades of clergy sexual misconduct, abuses of power, keeping secrets, all which Lindsey had worked to challenge by developing trust and building relationships among disparate parties. Now, Church leaders and Lindsey all needed fresh perspective, after eight years of fund-raising and contracting for over $3,000,000 in Capital improvements and major building construction, while rebuilding trust. Simultaneously, Lindsey had been planning to take a Sabbatical, marking his first 20 years in ministry. This Sabbatical was to be financed with $10,000 from his accrued wedding and funeral honorariums. His Sabbatical was to have been working intensively on conflict resolution, under the tutelage of Rev. Dr. "Speed" Leas, to envision the church, faith, ministry and life, differently. However, hours before meeting with David Bowman and the Sudanese on Valentine's Day, all the critical plans for what he would be doing on Sabbatical had been abandoned, due to the mentor having a heart attack.

Once the group had listened to Dr. Bowman, there was a prolonged uneasy silence at the table. After several moments, Rev. Lindsey leaned over to Steve Meyer with a suggestion, and Steve encouraged him to share the idea. Dr. Lindsey stated, "I do not want to presume, but I have the time and the resources. As pastor, I care about these men as if my own family. Could I go as your pastor, your representative, bearing your trust, the trust of your church? Could I go for you to your families?" Elder Jim Vedder later described to the Session of the church, "Who better could we have as our "ambassador of trust", than the pastor of the church, who has spent his life teaching us to trust amid the experience of brokenness? How better to experience and articulate conflict resolution than going to a war zone and listening for how trust is to be resurrected?" The primary purpose of this adventure was to find the families broken by war, and bring healing. Lindsey described in a sermon before leaving, "There is a parable of searching for the Lost Sheep, we are leaving the flock of the church together, searching for those who have been dispersed as the family of those called Lost Boys." Time was critical as this decision had been made mid-February and torrential seasonal rain had always begun mid-April. To have even two weeks in Sudan, they would need to leave America within six weeks, or be delayed six months, which if it were not possible would further delay construction of the Clinic at least a year.

So How Do You Get There?

John Dau had a cousin named Deng Leek, who planned to serve as Pastor Lindsey's traveling companion. In addition, Deng was a Philadelphia-based contractor, wanting to make in-roads in S. Sudan for his company. Rev. Lindsey planned to fly to London, then to Nairobi, Kenya, where the two would meet, and journey together through Africa. When the two flew from Nairobi to Lokichoggio, they planned to be met by Philip Thon Leek, John Dau's uncle, a Senator of the planned new government of Southern Sudan. In those few weeks, Lindsey began contacting any and every possibility for approval and guidance: Anglican Bishops, Presbyterian Missionaries, the US State Department, etc. without reply. Still, by contacting the Ministry of Health for Sudan, Dr. Marial Achol was willing to authorize Rev. Lindsey's Sabbatical to explore possibilities for building a clinic. With this Authorization as Letter of Invitation, Rev. Lindsey was assured he could go to the Sudanese People's Liberation Army Headquarters in Nairobi and acquire a Visa to travel in Southern Sudan and return.

Rev. Lindsey arranged for commercial travel to fly from Syracuse to Washington, DC, from the United States to London, England, then on to Nairobi, Kenya where he would spend the night. Then, he and Deng Leek would book passage and fly on a small commercial airline to Lokichoggio at the border of Kenya and Sudan; where they would then charter a private plane to take them to the Village of Pok Tap (Duk Padiet). There was one "known" obstacle, because the 25-year civil war had only just ended, there would be no banks or stores. All money for Rev. Lindsey's Sabbatical, commercial air tickets for he and Deng Leek to Lokichoggio, the cost of chartering a plane round trip to Southern Sudan, all food and gifts for the Village, had to be carried in cash. As the commercial describes "They don't take checks and they won't accept American Express." Cost for the round-trip charter was estimated to be $6,000 USD. In total, Rev. Lindsey took $20,000 in cash, most of which in new bills, hidden in various places on his body, for simplicity of less bills predominantly in new $100 bills. $10,000 of this from his wedding and funeral honoraria; $6,000 had been a gift from the Board of Directors of a local Foundation; $4,000 had been a gift from a couple in the congregation. Five thousand dollars of that $20,000 was hidden beneath the insole of each of his shoes; $5,000 was in a money belt under his clothes; $1,000 was in each breast pocket of his jacket; and $3,000 was divided up in his trousers pockets, so if robbed e could still have a security.

The week following Easter, on April 1st, 2005, arriving at Nairobi, Rev. Lindsey was the only American on the plane, the only Caucasian, as well as the only minister so wearing a clerical collar. He was a learned man with a doctorate; he had grown up in the cosmopolitan academic community of Ann Arbor, MI, gone to Seminary in Harlem, NY, he never thought himself biased by race, but suddenly to be the only white man was different. How different for a person to be a minority of one. To suddenly be a unique minority was dis-empowering and disconcerting, as he stood out, seeming to not belong and not be seen; and Nairobi was in a major city, what would it be like in the remote bush. On the plane, he had laughed to himself, "What is the worst that could happen?" John's cousin Deng would take care of things in Nairobi, John's uncle is a Senator whom we will meet before entering Sudan. But traveling into a war zone, did he even know where this village was located, and would it still be there?

Pastor, Trust No One, But Build Trust!

God's continuing sense of humor was at work, intervening in miraculous ways. John Dau and Paul Ariik had warned Rev. Lindsey prior to departure: "Nairobi is a very dangerous place of refugees. You cannot trust anyone. Especially not the Police or Taxi drivers, they are known to take tourists to remote destinations, to rob and kill them, and you will very visibly be alien." Stepping through Kenyan Customs, Deng Leek was nowhere to be found. Rev. Lindsey sat down on his backpack recognizing he was half-way around the world with no interpreter, no companion for the journey, no understanding of exactly where he was going, and a stern warning from the Sudanese Refugees to TRUST NO ONE. Lindsey wondered, what was God Calling him to do by taking all these elements away, leaving him alone? Who was he to think that he could represent Sudanese refugees in Africa? Who was he to represent trust? He felt vulnerable having so much money on his body in large bills? What good would money do?

Suddenly, entering the airport, there was a crowd of 10 Sudanese, chanting, singing, carrying a large sign that read "DUK LOST BOY: LINDSEY". They surrounded him as Lindsey realized, now I have become the Lost Boy. They took $3,000 of Rev. Lindsey's cash, everything in his trouser pockets, converting this to Kenyan Shillings, to hire two taxis to take the group to the Mayfield Guest House. All the while Rev. Lindsey wondered about "trust," wondered about these companions who suddenly had claimed him, and had spent his money for him. He wondered where Deng Leek might be, if he had made a mistake in coming, a mistake that might risk his life.

There are two overnight accommodations called "Mayfield" within the City of Nairobi. The Mayfield (Hilton) Hotel is a $200 /night International hotel. The Mayfield Guest House, is a hostel used by African Inland Missionaries

(AIM) at $20 /night, located next to the City Morgue and Cemetery. Eventually finding the Mayfield Guest House, in private Rev. Paul Majok explained that Deng Leek's mother had died; Deng had come home for the funeral, and now returned to America, so he would no longer be traveling to Pok Tap. Lindsey was all alone.

Rev. Paul Majok then searched Lindsey's face as he raised a different question about trust. Rev. Paul Majok identified himself as The Anglican Priest for Pok Tap, who because of the war, had made his home in Nairobi. "So, who was Rev. Lindsey, as an American Minister, going into his parish, without his invitation?" Rev. Lindsey described he had tried to contact the Presbyterian Missionaries and the Anglican Bishops for the area, but they had not responded. Paul Majok said he knew all about those contacts, that his Bishops had DECLINED Rev. Lindsey coming by not responding, yet here he was. Now Rev. Majok had his own decision to make. His Bishop had refused Rev. Lindsey by avoidance, rather than explicitly directing Lindsey not come. Rev. Majok personally knew John Dau and Paul Ariik as having been age mates, born in the same village; Jacob Majok was Rev. Paul Majok's cousin. These Sudanese refugees in America were doing this to benefit their village, his parish, their family. So, he and Rev. Lindsey would each need to spend the night praying what they were to do. Lindsey wondered at this territorial behavior, then realized how protective he felt about the parish he served, and the rights he had concerning other ministers providing weddings, funerals, baptisms in his home congregation.

In the morning, Rev. Lindsey used the satellite mobile phone he brought to phone Dr. Achol at the Ministry of Health, learning Dr. Achol had gone to the city of Rumbeck, but his assistant "Kennedy" would take Rev. Lindsey to the SPLA Headquarters for an SPLA Visa. They arrived at 9:30am. Kennedy spoke to men gathered there, who said the Secretary was on coffee break, and when she returned she would process his Visa for his plane's 3pm departure. The two waited. At 11am Kennedy needed to leave for another appointment, and Lindsey sat uncomfortably waiting, all the while recalling "This is Africa" time is different, just wait and trust that God will work everything out. After four hours of waiting, at 1:30pm the Secretary walked in, quite frustrated that someone would dare want immediate action. She described that the process for getting a Visa usually took two weeks, but in that he had letters from the Ministry of Health and Senator Philip Thon Leek of the SPLM, he had photos for the Visa, and $50 in American currency; if he had an additional $50 for her to waive the waiting period, she would make an exception for him. Lindsey recalled the original advice from David Bowman regarding a modicum of graft and decided this was worth the price.

Flying Solo, Are You Carrying Anything for Anyone...

Rev. Lindsey arrived at Wilson Airport at 2:00pm for the 3:00pm flight; which in turn did not depart until 4:30pm (TIA). As he got his backpack out of the taxi, Rev. Paul Majok came walking up to Lindsey all smiles, saying that in his prayers Jesus had come to him. Jesus said that he should go along with Rev. Lindsey, assisting Rev. Lindsey like Barnabas with Paul, because Deng would not be coming. He could serve as Rev. Lindsey's guide in Rev. Majok's parish, <u>provided</u> Rev. Lindsey assisted by paying all costs, this included $300 per round trip ticket from Nairobi to Lokichoggio, all meals and housing at Lokichoggio ($200 for each person), snacks, water and juice $25-30 /each. Rev. Paul Majok's "generosity," in accepting Christ's call to

accompany Rev. Lindsey, was going to cost Rev. Lindsey a minimum of $1,050 and that would only be the beginning. Would God's Calling of the Church of the Western World, be only to finance change and ministry in this distant land? Lindsey wondered at the distinction between charitable giving versus personal engagement and action, when describing mission.

While waiting for the plane to leave, Rev. Paul Majok described his Sudan, Duk County, the families torn apart by war, and the great importance of building a Clinic. He then described, that in addition to the refugees' dream of providing health care, he also had a dream. Lindsey felt like a captive audience, recognizing he might need to fulfill Rev. Majok's dream, and finance a Clinic, all to reunite lost and broken families after 20 years of Civil War. He questioned his own motivations about charity and mission, and trust. Rev. Majok's dream was of having oxen and plows owned by the church, that would be used as a cultivation co-op. Rev. Paul described that while this is a cattle culture, cattle are revered and never put to work. People were literally crawling on their hands and knees, digging with their hands to bury a single seed, then scratching the earth at another location to bury the next. If his church could own oxen and plows, then the church could plow people's fields, empowering them to feed themselves and the community cooperatively. Did Rev. Lindsey believe he was called to help his friend in this way?

At Lokichoggio (Loki), Rev. Lindsey and Rev. Majok were not met by Senator Philip Thon Leek, but instead by another of John's uncles Martin Deng Leek, along with Rosemary Nwanga of the Norwegian Peoples' AID organization (NPA). NPA had handled all logistics and humanitarian support of the Southern Sudanese people throughout the +20 years of war. Rosemary had arranged for a private plane for them to charter, for flying the following day. They went into the small office, and were presented a contract that described round trip flight from Lokichoggio to Pok Tap, but surprisingly the cost was $3,000 instead of the $6,000 they had originally been quoted. Rev. Lindsey questioned the difference, and asked "This is round trip?" to which everyone agreed. Not one to poison a good deal, Rev. Lindsey retrieved three thousand dollars from his shoe, causing everyone to laugh, then signed the contract with a date for his pick-up in Sudan. Lokichoggio was a bare flat location at the base of an escarpment. There were soldiers wandering about, and several different charter plane companies. Rev. Lindsey took a photo of the place; immediately he was surrounded by armed soldiers, who identified that this has been a United Nations site for transporting food and humanitarian aid throughout each of the wars in various African nations. Photos might compromise that location for future use. Enormous Goliath transport planes landed and took off, shaking everything in their vicinity.

They drove to the NPA compound, a series of cement block huts with thatched roofs. Rev. Majok described that there was a refugee from Kakuma Camp who also wanted to "catch a ride with them", which seemed an odd expression for air travel, but "This is Africa". Lindsey smiled to himself, that supposedly Rev. Paul had only come to the idea of accompanying Lindsey to Sudan that day, yet waiting for them at Loki was a refugee from the camp 2 days away by bicycle, whom Majok had promised a ride. The following morning at the airport, Solomon greeted them smiling, sitting atop several bags of seed, and boxes of used clothing. Not the baggage Lindsey had anticipated, but "This Is Africa." Solomon seemed like Lot's son in the Book of Genesis, accompanying Abraham into the wilderness.

Rosemary then asked Rev. Lindsey to accompany her, alone. He had a sense of foreboding as he recalled the advice to trust no one, yet his role was to personify developing trust. The two went into a small metal shed, with a locked door and no windows. At the center of the room was a card table, atop which was a 12" square cardboard box and clipboard. Rosemary explained that NPA had been unable to pay their personnel for quite some time, years in fact. This box represented salaries of people he would be working with, and his serving as courier would help solidify trust. She presented a manifest, identifying who was to receive how much. At the bottom of the last page was a total line in Kenyan Shillings and conversion to the amount "$3,000,000 United States Currency." Lindsey signed the sheet of notebook paper, and accepted the box. Martin Leek and Rev. Paul Majok offered to take the odd box to give to Solomon, or to put in the back with the rest of the luggage, but Rev. Lindsey insisted he would hold onto this one for the six-hour flight. As they flew over the desert, Rev. Lindsey wondered what he had gotten into. Could this be money for weapons, drugs, bribes? What could be done with $3,000,000? Rev. Lindsey remembered the $20,000 he had been carrying. He also remembered the letters he had been asked to carry by refugees in America. He wondered how many of the letters carried dowry for marriages, and money for family members. He wondered how much he was now carrying? He recalled the airline agent in America, who had routinely asked, "Has anyone given you anything to carry for them?" What kind of reaction might he have gotten had he presented her the $3,000,000 box and then begun pulling $30,000 more in wads of new $100 bills from every pocket and shoe? He realized he would not have gotten this far, or been given so much trust, if he had. The words of the conclusion of the Parable of the Talents resounded in his mind's ear "Well done good and faithful servant. You have been faithful over a little, I will set you over much." Trust suddenly became very expensive and very dangerous.

The topography of the Rift Valley quickly turned from Lokichoggio's escarpment, to crater lakes atop volcanoes, to vast open desert as far as they eye could see.

For hours, they flew over parched dry wasteland. Occasionally, there were herds of water buffalo, elephants, zebra. Rev. Lindsey was surprised how much the view beneath them looked like the relief map on globes of Africa. After several hours, the pilot radioed to the village, that they would be landing. Beneath was a small outcropping of low trees and thatched huts. The Villagers radioed back to wait, as cattle were grazing on the runway. The plane touched down, and as the passengers stepped out, they were greeted by the whole village, singing, beating a bass drum. Michael India introduced himself as the local head of the NPA and that Rev. Lindsey had a package for him. Michael took the box and quickly disappeared. The Village leaders paraded passed the huts to a large metal roof supported on 12-foot steel uprights, with no walls or floor, everyone singing. The scene seemed reminiscent of Palm Sunday, with a triumphal entry, that seemed somehow pregnant with fear of what might happen.

Lindsey felt he had stepped into a different world, a foreigner in a foreign land, a man of God entering God's Creation. It was dry, so dry the ground had cracked open, the earth was hard packed sand, and breezes whipped little whirlwinds of biting sand. Semi-trailer cargo containers had been converted into residences, the steel dwellings looked like ovens. Heavy construction equipment, cranes, bulldozers, trucks were dispersed all throughout the village, yet they were long neglected, covered in rust and decay . Village leaders described that, contractors creating a canal wider than the Suez, had set their equipment on fire to seize the motors, making them obstacles instead of tools. Few images could have portrayed more poignantly that the population had only recently returned, than the evidence of an entire village of people living during 25 years of war's refuge and arrogant waste. There were also identifications of where unexploded bombs had landed, and to stay away from these. One of the companions said, "Go nowhere without us and you will be safe."

Rev. Paul made introductions and offered a prayer of greeting. The temperature was over 120 degrees, and everyone stared at the stranger in black shirt and white clerical collar. Rev. Paul Majok explained that: "I possess a gift for the Village. The people had heard of white people, and they had seen Rev. Majok and other clergy in a collar, but they had never imagined a White man could be a Priest! Rev. Majok had brought this "White Priest" as a gift!"

Rev. Lindsey described that he had come on behalf of their sons and daughters in America, many of whom, they thought dead, but were alive and well. He identified having photos and letters that Michael India would distribute to those they belonged. Rev. Lindsey identified that he also had brought a camera, and with their permission would be taking their photos to share with their sons and daughters in America. From the church, everyone was dismissed, as the travelers were taken to their huts to settle in. His companions explained that to bathe, there was an oil drum which had been filled with water from the pond. He could dip from this with a coffee can to take a sponge bath, as water in the dry season is extremely precious. For

bodily waste, he was to dig a hole in the sand with his hand, squat, then cover the sand as deep as possible.

Initial Plans to Create a Clinic

A short time later that afternoon, word came that the Village Chiefs had gathered for a presentation and discussion. This is a tribal culture, where everything is verbal, and a person's word is their bond. The Dinka are a family based tribal culture, where every person (male, though when invited a woman could be asked to speak) has a voice, and their voice becomes their vote. This is not a Democracy with majority rule, or a Monarchy with Royal decree.

North American "decision-making" culture is heavily laden with assumptions based on Roberts' Rules of Order. Roberts had been a Calvary Captain wounded in the Spanish American War. While convalescing, Roberts wrote down a method for conflict resolution during war. Different from a Monarchy, where only the royalty could make decisions, Roberts Rules gave equal rights and authority to all citizens/members and were planned based on persons invested and involved being able to speak, to debate, to convince an accepted majority to resolve, or to appeal decisions. Yet a third paradigm of decision making, is that attributed to the Quakers, of non-anxious waiting in prayer and silence until the Holy Spirit has convinced the body of a unanimous decision.

In the Dinka culture, if there is disagreement, even a single voice, nothing can occur until everyone is convinced to agree. When there is disagreement, an elder is often conscripted whom both accept, and will trust to arbitrate. Much like the Old Testament book of Judges, the role of the Village Chief is as Judge in legal disputes, to determine right and wrong, God's will, and punishment within the tribe. However, in a community that has been at war for over 20 years, where every male over the age of twelve carries an AK47, every woman and child has a machete, often the offended do not wait for arrest and trial, and changing to an ordered society will be difficult. Living at Level Four Conflict, de-escalation of fear and increasing trust does not come easily. In many ways, this culture is reminiscent of the American Wild West, just as high illiteracy, just as high rate of disease; clean water and grazing land for cattle the only priority. The primary difference, being that instead of a six shooter in a holster, their guns were automatic weapons.

David, an Outreach Worker from Sudan Medical Care (SMC), made a thorough presentation of the Health Care circumstance, and lack thereof.

SMC described that the primary problem is due to the rural nature of this community, there are no accurate statistical information, everything is anecdotal. Second, third and fourth, this people have suffered the effects of war, poverty, irresponsible government. There has been no surgical services, no maternal/child services, no nutritional guide, no immunizations for preventable diseases. Added to these problems, this region is landlocked during rainy seasons. In the incidence of appendicitis, or gunshot wounds, a person is isolated and dies. Leading causes of death are lack of pre-natal care, diarrhea, and lack of post-natal care. There is a critical need for a Referral Hospital at Duk Payuel and Primary Health Care Clinic at Duk Pajut (Pok Tap). These became the purposes of a clinic.

There is need for a Census, to begin to track statistics, however this will be complicated by several factors...

• Refugees are returning daily. The United Nations is "re-patriating" 150 to this community per day. Giving them a blanket and handful of seed, and good wishes, knowing that they may not remain here. In 2005, at Rev. Lindsey's visit, there were 700 people at Pok Tap, but historically this had been a region with 45,300 people. Duk Payuel itself had once had 36,500 people; in 2005 there was one man living there, with his wife and infant son.

• Typically, a Census is tracked by the male head of household, but in a polygamous culture a man could have several wives and families.

• With mud huts and no postal service, there are no individual addresses or residence.

• Being a nomadic people the whole village sometimes moves for the benefit of the cattle or to evade war.

• The Outreach Health Care workers described the priority of health care during pregnancy as the population had an extremely high incidence of death among mothers and their children during

delivery. Lindsey acknowledged that he could identify with this, as his own mother had died during his birth and delivery. It was a simple and straight forward personal connection, but for the community, this identified with their suffering. Lindsey also shared that he had training in community development and wondered what planning they had done for development? The leaders scoffed, saying "We want development, no matter what, no matter where, we need."

Rev. Lindsey had brought along with him two doctor's medical equipment bags, as gifts from the Welch/Allyn corporation, which contained stethoscopes, otoscopes and blood pressure cuffs, both for adults and for infants. The outreach workers had never seen equipment sized for infant children and were extremely thankful.

Entrusted with A Name for John Doe

The Village Chiefs then asked how Rev. Lindsey knew John Dau. The pastor described that before leaving the United States, he had said goodbye to John Dau at the airport, and in order to hug him had had to stand on tiptoe. Everyone laughed, but recognized the reference to the height of John's family.

At this point, The Dinka Tribal Chief of the Village of Pok Tap (Duk Pajut) stood up, whose name was Daniel Deng Leek. Daniel Deng Leek explained, this is not a story usually told in public, but this is a special occasion: a homecoming for a stranger who had come in the name of their lost sons. Chief Daniel Deng Leek described that when he was young he had fallen in love. He had taken the woman as his bride, and they had a child. But when the child was born, her brother, the infant's uncle, came saying that the dowry had not been satisfied, so he (the brother) was to name the baby instead of the child's father, and this baby was called by the uncle, John Dau. Years later, Daniel Deng Leek had fulfilled the dowry, and wanted to name his son with a fitting name, but the war had come and they had been separated from their child, believing the son had died. "Reverend when you return to your home, and to my son, I ask that you have a great feast with a heifer, at which time, you call my son forward and present to him the name of "Jacob Dhieu Deng Leek Magaar".

"Dhieu" means crying, because when he was a child, ALL the people cried because of the suffering and oppression, then he was taken from us and we cried, but now he is restored and we cry different tears. "Deng" is a very common Dinka name, meaning that it was raining when the child was born, and for nine months every year, it rains. "Magaar" is the Dinka tribal name for a straight horned bull of long horns. When the child had lived in the Village, he had loved a long horned bull. "Leek" was their family name.

Rev. Lindsey recognized he had come bearing the name of John Dau as his introduction, yet he would return bearing a new name for his friend, the sacred name of "Jacob Dhieu Deng Leek Magaar" for one who had been dead, as the son of the chief / brought back to life, and a John Doe who now was known and claimed.

Rev. Lindsey affirmed that he had come on behalf of all their sons and daughters in America, who now wanted to do a great thing, because they wanted to give their families the medical care of a doctor and midwife through a clinic.

Part 3

Developing Covenant Relationships in Sudan

Supreme Dinka Chief Chuiee Deng Leek then rose to his feet. He spoke quietly, but with stern tones. He said that, "What the good reverend has offered is a great thing, if this should come to be, the reverend and his family and church would be blessed with great blessings and long life. BUT, we are a people who have suffered much, and we have suffered because many others have made promises they never fulfilled. SO, if this promise is not fulfilled, the reverend and all he knows and cares for would be cursed and die a miserable death." Many in the community laughed with embarrassment, but Chief Chuiee and Rev. Lindsey stared into each other's eyes a long time, then Supreme Chief Chuiee tapped the reverend on the chest above his heart, and walked away.

Everyone left the place of meeting and walked to the site of the Canal. This construction project had been promised and never finished. In its construction, many had died, many animals had had their migration patterns permanently changed, whole herds had drowned. At the outbreak of war, the contractors had abandoned cranes and bulldozers, setting their engines afire so they would seize up and could not be used. These behemoths stood like statues of death, to uncompleted promises. The people crossed over the dry canal bed 100 yards wide, and over the opposite bank stood a clinic building. Supreme Chief Chuiee described that CARE International had promised this clinic five years before, but it was never completed. For the first years, the ground stood vacant, then they began to build, then they stopped. Recently, with the knowledge that an American was coming to build a clinic, the contractors had worked to put on a roof, and put up internal walls, but this clinic had been another promise that was unfulfilled.

Beginning on Sunday Morning

During the night, Rev. Lindsey slept fitfully. At one point, he was awakened by a series of loud sounds, though he knew not what. The next morning was Sunday. As the Village came to life and the sun and heat rose, Rev. Lindsey knew he was in trouble. He felt feverish, cold sweat though at dawn the air temperature was already over 120 degrees. The smells of cook fires, cattle and burning cow dung made the air thick. Michael India explained that during the night, a man had come to his wife's hut and found another man there. While this is a polygamous culture for men to have more than one wife, a woman could only have one husband. The new laws for the new Sudan, give responsibility for such a case to the Chief as Judge, but this man had exercised his own justice by shooting both his wife and her lover. Breakfast was chi, a boiled milk tea, served with deep fried pieces of dough. Immediately, Lindsey became violently ill and had difficulty standing. Rev. Paul Majok greeted him with great smiles, describing that people had come from all the surrounding villages to welcome him home and to see the White American Reverend. Now was the time to worship God.

Unsteadily they walked to the Church, where close to 3,000 people had already gathered in the 120-degree heat. Rev. Paul Majok was dressed head to foot in black, over this he then donned black robes, and covered this with a white alb. People from the surrounding villages had walked throughout the night together to be present for this special worship service. Early in the worship service, Pastor Peter described what had happened the night before, and how the blood from two members of their village had now joined that of their ancestors, being absorbed into the earth. One of the family members knelt and allowed a stream of sand to pour through his fingers.

Rev. Lindsey had brought a pottery communion cup and plate for the church, as well as a Bible, both of which he presented ceremonially to Rev. Peter. The children's choirs from each individual church provided an anthem complete with dancing. Rev. Paul described that prior to their conversion to Christianity, the bass drum had been used to symbolize the beating of an animal's heart as it was sacrificed, and the power of the bull's blood was used to wash away the sins of people as they were bathed in blood. When they became Christians, they painted a cross on the side of the drum in bull's blood, and still in Christian worship, this was the principle musical instrument. A visiting deacon from another Anglican Church was invited to preach "the first sermon", and she described that in New Sudan, women would have equal roles of leadership and human rights with men. Suddenly, tape recorders appeared, and the congregation began singing to the chanted music on the boom boxes.

Rev. Lindsey was then invited to preach "the second sermon". He read to the congregation from Isaiah 40, with Rev. Paul Majok translating phrase by phrase into Dinka, "Comfort, comfort, my people, says your God." Lindsey described the painful irony, that since arriving he had repeatedly heard them reference themselves, as "The Suffering People of South Sudan", yet their children, whom he knew in the Diaspora of America, cling to the image that this is "home" and home is a place rich in memory and blessings.

He named that the media had drawn attention to their plight, by naming the children refugees at Kakuma and elsewhere as "The Lost Boys", but this title is wrong. Jesus rarely referred to people as "sinners", but often as "lost", like the Lost sheep and Lost coin, meaning that they had sought their own way, apart from God; and this was not true of their sons and daughters. He professed that he knew, and their children knew, they were never Lost from God; they were Never Lost from the love and memory of their village, and while these had been children at the start of the war, they had matured into men, so instead of "Lost Boys" Rev. Lindsey professed, that he had known their sons and daughters, as his own brothers and family. His joy today was in returning that which the parents had thought was lost, but had instead been hidden by God, until this time and for bringing a new thing, grace, forgiveness and resurrection to New Sudan.

Rev. Lindsey then knelt on his knees and he took up a handful of earthy sand, he rose to stand and taking a pinch of this in his other hand, placed the soil in his mouth and swallowed, allowing the remainder of the sand to fall dramatically from between his fingers. All the while, as preacher he described that for generations, back to the Biblical Garden this people had been born and lived and died in this place, their lives were in this earth, just as Rev. Peter had said earlier of the blood of this couple and all their ancestors being absorbed into this sand. Rev. Lindsey swallowed again, claiming that they and their ancestors were now part of him, part of his life forever, never lost, never forgotten, but redeemed and restored through their relationship.

Rev. Lindsey concluded by telling a story from over 100 years ago in the history of his Church in America. At one point, there had been a fist fight between two leaders of the Church. Afterwards, the Church was divided in loyalty between the two. For five years, the pastor had served both Churches, as they worshiped separately and met separately, each claiming to be the true Church under that name. The only record that they have of that time, is that in their history there are torn out pages from the binding. In the notation on the next page, is description that the Church had come to realize that by their divisions they had wounded God, they had torn apart and crucified the Lord and Savior Jesus Christ. They repented of the harm they had done to one another, to the Church and to God, so they had torn out those pages of their history, and begun again. Rev. Lindsey then gave to Pastor Peter a large hard covered bound book with blank pages for writing their history, and he tore out the first several pages, stating that their history as a Church began again, knowing there had been suffering, there had been war and loss, but our purpose now is to gather and to build.

The worship service had already gone on for three hours in 120-degree extreme heat, and Rev. Lindsey was now quite ill, light headed, feverish and weak. All the honored guests were excused, as Rev. Paul Majok concluded the service with prayers and benediction. The twelve local Anglican and Presbyterian clergy then invited Rev. Lindsey to come away with them. Unsteadily, he walked along beside new friends, hoping he could keep up without passing out. About a mile outside the Village, they sat beneath a tree.

Rev. Lindsey had brought necklace crosses for each, every cross unique, and he made a point to personally give these to each.

He listened as they described that none of them, not Pastor Peter, not Rev. Paul Majok, none, had ever gone to school, let alone to theological seminary, and as an American pastor with years of experience, with degrees in theology, they trusted him to listen, to be their elder, to hear their confessions and to pray for their pastoral concerns for them. For four hours, the pastors described caring for people during the long years of civil war. Each described their lack of training or understanding, reaching ever deeper into their faith in God, their compassion and building one personal experience upon another. They described how many of their wives and families were in refugee camps or hospitals, how many had become ill with mental problems and stress. They named their fears, their worries and their doubts. Rev. Lindsey listened to each, and helped them to listen to one another, periodically leading them in prayer together, regularly affirming the ministry they had done and the faith implicit in their words and actions. He modeled clergy caring for each other as confessor and the power of small groups to minister. Based on one story, he offered a Bible lesson. Based on another, he offered understanding, forgiveness and compassion. He wondered what professors: Cone, Trible, Brueggemann, Forbes would think? At one point, Rev. Paul stated, "We would like for this sharing to go on throughout the night, but it appears you would like to be on your way." Rev. Lindsey tried to smile, saying "I treasure the time we have spent together, but I feel so very ill, I am afraid I am going to die!" The clergy quickly took him up, placing his arms over their shoulders, they walked back to the Village, they brought his mat and mosquito netting out to lay on the ground in the shadow of the hut.

David, a NPA staff member took a red towel and soaked it in water, then placed this over Rev. Lindsey's head, neck and shoulders. During the rainy season 14 inches of rain fell each day, but during the three months of dry season the ground cracked with drought. The only immediate source of water were stagnant ponds, from which a used 500-gallon diesel oil drum would be filled. The water smelled of petroleum, and stagnation, yet the cool damp cloth helped revive him, as the red dye from the towel leached out staining all his clothes and skin with the color of blood.

Outreach workers were called, who, using the Medical Kit Rev. Lindsey had just brought, took his blood pressure and vital signs, diagnosing he had heat prostration and electrolyte imbalance, which untreated would be fatal. They described how serious this was, and that they had a chemical that he should mix with three liters of water and drink, forcing another three liters down that night and again for the next three days. The mixture tasted horrible of raw salts and potassium, but he could literally feel the salts and bodily fluids of his flesh re-absorbing like a sponge. Surely, this is what the Cup of Communion was supposed to represent. Having tasted death and brokenness, literally feeling the bitter drink replenish our being. Instead, Churches have fought over whether grape juice or fermented wine. Weak and exhausted, the American Reverend lay on his mat on the ground as the sun set.

The next morning, he awoke to discover Rev. Paul kneeling by his bedside. Rev. Paul described that one time during the night, Rev. Craig had rolled over in a dream, but otherwise he had slept peacefully. Rev. Paul had stayed by his bedside all through the night, praying for his strength and recovery. For the next three days, Rev. Lindsey lay ill, rising to make appearances and do whatever needed to be done, while trying to regain his strength.

On that first Monday, the Commissioner of Duk County was "in residence" at Pok Tap and an audience was arranged for Rev. Lindsey to meet with the Commissioner, "His Excellence, John Daum". According to the design for the new government Duk County would be composed of six "payams", Duk Payuel being one, Pok Tap (Duk Pajut) being a second. The County Commissioner had determined they had need for 4 Primary Health Care Centers (Referral Hospitals), 6 Primary Health Care Units (Clinics), Ambulances for transport, 4 Health Care Outreach Workers, 40 new Bore wells for water free of disease, and Public Health Education.

Rev. Lindsey said he represented no one with money, but only their own sons and daughters who had survived the diaspora deportation, had come to America and now wanted to help, by creating one Clinic. They would try to work to complete this one clinic, and after that is followed through, then they would see where they were for additional projects. His Excellence John Daum stated that Dinka culture insists "We are not requesting you do anything, we are pointing out our needs for you."

That afternoon, Rev. Paul Majok, Pastor Peter, Michael India and Rev. Lindsey, met together. Lindsey described the dream Rev. Paul Majok had shared of having oxen and plows owned by the Church as a co-op for farming cultivation. Rev. Lindsey then asked Michael India to serve as witness, as he gave Rev. Peter and Rev. Paul $3,000 to make this dream a reality. They thanked him for his trust and generosity, describing that this gift would allow them to purchase and train 10 oxen with five plows. In the future, this would make a great change in their community.

Late in the day, Paramount Dinka Chief Chuiee Deng Leek and Chief Daniel Deng Leek, along with traveling companion Martin Deng Leek and Rev.

Lindsey, then sat together. Rev. Lindsey described that as his hosts, he had a gift for these brothers. He described that many things in life are consumables, they are needed for the sustenance of life and nothing more. But there is also a gift, an unmerited unexpected act of grace, that allows you to change a circumstance, to create a business or invest in people. He then gave to the Chiefs, a gift from his own funds of $1,000. They were visibly moved, both by the explanation and the magnitude of the gift.

Two days later, they described they had gathered their family members to discuss what should be done with this gift. They discussed sewing machines that could start a business, seed that could be planted. Then they named another son, who had fallen in love with a girl in Nairobi and he had been driving a taxi. The car had broken down and he had gotten into trouble with the Police, the woman had abandoned him, he was lost and in prison. They agreed that this gift, could pay for his freedom from the police, his return to his family, and the opportunity for him to become the taxi driver between Duk Payuel and Pok Tap.

Rev. Lindsey spent the afternoon talking with Michael India, who described that in Africa everything has multiple names, in part because of multiple languages but also for multiple identities, and his name is also Majur Aleer. Michael's grandfathers had been the Tribal Witch Doctors. As a youth, he had gone to school in the north, but instead of becoming Muslim, he had become a Sudanese Christian. Michael returned home in 1978 and spent forty days and forty nights with his grandfather, telling his elder all about Christianity and the love of God in Jesus Christ who never forgot the covenant. Together, Michael and his grandfather decided to overturn the stones of the shrine and dismantle the altar for animal sacrifices beneath the three tall Palm trees, at which point Michael baptized his grandfather, and together the two of them baptized the entire tribe. Michael was born in 1967, so this had all taken place when he was 11 years of age.

About 5:00pm lorries arrived to transport Rev. Lindsey, Michael India, Chief Daniel Deng Leek and his brother Supreme Chief Chuiee Deng Leek, Rev. Paul Majok, Pastor Peter, and three gun carrying soldiers to Duk Payuel.

Standing beneath the three tall Palm trees, where Michael described the tribe had long held a sacred shrine and altar for sacrifice, the "Two Chiefs of the Two Duks", Paramount Chief Chiuee Deng Leek and Chief Daniel Deng Leek declared "For the whole Joint Council we offer land at Duk Payuel for the Duk Lost Boys Clinic. If you do not fulfill this, if you and our sons do not return, you will be liars and will bring shame upon us all." In so far as community land ownership in the new nation being formed was still undecided, this land was considered as an "inheritance", given by the whole community, owned by the community, without cost. Choice of building style was important, because traditional dwellings had all been temporary, made of purged mud and branches, with a thatched roof, constructed in a circle with round walls. The Clinic would be visibly different. This would be a permanent building, made of brick and mortar to outlast the pyramids of Egypt, rectangular with screened windows, a metal roof, electric light, and they would need reliable communication.

The site needed to be level for the pouring of a concrete floor. The site needed to be high ground with adequate drainage, due to the rainy season. The site needed to be near the village, yet enough distant to be able to be quarantined or identified in an emergency. The site needed clean water from an isolated bore hole that would be sealed to prevent animal contamination, and a landing strip for evacuation of patients. There also would be questions of what direction to orient the building, as village huts all faced one another in a common hub. The Village of Duk Payuel had been an historic tribal Capital Village, known and recognized by people, identified with worship as the place for sacrifices. During the early 1900s this had been an official Village with the residence of a British administrator. The only evidence of those days was a rusting elevated water tank. They sat beneath this, as a landmark for the rebuilding of Duk with clean water and a clinic for health care.

Sitting beneath the elevated tank, they met the Dinka Elder named Gideon, who was the primary resident of the Village. Gideon told how he had been captured by the Northern army after being shot. They attempted to scalp him by pealing the skin from his head. But he had gotten free and had killed three soldiers with rocks. Gideon appeared to be advanced in age, white haired with a beard. With pride, he introduced his wife, who was perhaps 17 and pregnant, and their toddler who hung on her ankle. "We are the first family at Duk, like Adam and Eve. There are 46 cows here at Duk Payuel. Tell the Sons of Duk, there are again cattle at Duk Payuel. Then they will be very happy."

Returning to the Village of Pok Tap that night, stories of the war were told, along with the costs of peace. Another of John Dau's uncles was a General in the military of the SPLA, named Thor Thon Leek. Thor Thon Leek took Lindsey off about 200 yards by themselves, together they stared at the stars in the dark of night. Thor Thon Leek stood 6 foot 9 inches, with hard features, bright attentive eyes, he always wore uniform and a beret, a pistol on one hip and machete on the other. Thor Thon Leek suddenly took out the machete and held it to the pastor's throat, he then used the blade to draw a line down his sternum to his midsection. Lindsey dared not move as this warrior described "I wish I could cut you and remove all your organs, to put children in this body. That is the only way these children have a chance, for someone to take them to America." Then Thor Thon Leek laughed a deep belly laugh and holding Lindsey by the shoulder proclaimed, "But we do not kill friends!" Suddenly, Lindsey realized just how dangerous and desperate were the circumstances, and how desperate the people for a different life for their children.

Thor Thon Leek had a tone of sadness and regret as he then inquired, "As long as anyone has been alive, we were one people. We have been Sudanese of Duk. Now there are Sudanese in America. There are people from Duk in many different places. There are Sudanese people Sudanese in Europe, there are Sudanese in Australia. There are people of Duk who were taken to the North, and brainwashed. How can we ever again be one from Duk?" When Rev. Lindsey realized Thor was waiting for an answer, he attempted to find his voice, and Rev. Lindsey prophesied, "It took a hundred years for this war to occur, and over 20 years for the war to be fought, all while children were dispersed in this Diaspora. It will take time, but we will develop trust, we will become partners to again become one. That is the hope and promise of communion."

The final night of Rev. Lindsey's tour, another of the Chiefs of a Payam, came to visit in the dark, reminiscent of the visit of the Pharisee Nicodemus. This leader asked, "My son is in America. Is my son behaving with respect, or is he bringing shame upon our family?" Regardless of culture or century, parents always worry about their children. Rev. Lindsey assured the Chief that his son was a good son, who would bring only honor to his father and his people.

Rev. Lindsey was then asked by one person after another, "When will you return to Duk?" He confessed, "I came now because your sons and daughters could not, they did not yet have visas and passports to travel safely so soon after the end of the war. So, I came to you, to represent them. The next visitors that come, I hope and pray will be the return of your loved ones. And after that, the building of the Clinic." Chief Daniel Deng Leek described, "Our sons are in America with your family, and you are here with us. You have been faithful so you are our family, and your people are our people." Rev. Lindsey quoted the book of Ruth, "And from now on, where you go I shall go, your Village shall be one with my Village, your people shall be my people, your God and my God are one; where you die, my heart will die and there will I be buried. May the Lord do so to me and more also, if even death parts us from one another."

As Lindsey prepared to leave, a woman came to him and through an interpreter said to him, "I have no one and nothing. Everything was lost to me in the war. Give me something from America. It need not be much, but it will be from you, from America, that I must hold, until you return." Rev. Lindsey thought he had given away everything he thought he had. He quickly went through his pockets and found he still had one crumpled five-dollar bill. In Sudan, the only money that is considered of any worth, is in large denominations and of recent minting. In 2005, $100 bills from the year 2000 or more recent had value, anything of the 20th Century or older, or of smaller value was worthless, because they had known so many revolutions where smaller bills and older bills had lost all value. He gave the woman a used $5 bill, dated 1976.

The next day, they rose early in the morning and waited all day for the plane to appear, but it did not. After many hours, they used the radio in the lorries to contact another lorry, to contact another lorry, to contact another lorry, eventually to contact the airport. The charter airline at the airport stated, "We have no record of you flying out." Rev. Lindsey became concerned he might never return, as he heard voices echo in his memory "trust no one". He described, "But, we signed a contract for a round trip flight." The Charter air company responded in the affirmative, "Yes, pilot flew you in, and pilot had returned to the airport, one round trip." He recalled the words of Dr. David Bowman, that in Africa contracts count for nothing, all that matters are relationships of trust. Rev. Lindsey inquired what it would cost to now fly him and his party out, and the agent said "$4,000". Rev. Lindsey recognized this is the way things are done in Africa (TIA), but he had given his extra money as gifts: To Rural Deacon Elijah for the Church's agricultural program, for Daniel Deng Leek's son to get out of jail in Nairobi, even the $5 to the woman. He could not possibly ask for the return of these gifts. So, he began negotiation bartering with the air charter company, through six radio operators each positioned in their lorries. When they reached $3,000, he realized this was what he had originally anticipated paying, and he still had this amount, so called for the plane to come. However, you could smell the rain coming, the heat intensified as it seemed the rain's cold front was pushing the hot air more intensely. Suddenly the skies opened after four months, and within one hour, sixteen inches of rain had fallen. There were standing pools of water atop the packed sand. When the rain relented for the day, they recognized they could not use the tiny airstrip on which they had landed. They would need to drive to Mareng to meet the plane, and to drive to Mareng meant leaving the compound at three in the morning.

Another of John Dau's uncles arrived, this one with a wife, describing that they needed to be taken to Mareng, so they would share the Lorries. The couple slept in the bed of the pick-up truck, as Rev. Lindsey dragged his mattress out beneath the stars a final night. Never had he seen so many stars, even away from cities in rural areas of America, still there had been some light, and here without any electric power, so close to the equator, the sky was awesome. At three a.m., everyone was sitting in the back of the pick-up truck with their luggage.

Martin asked if any belongings had been left. Rev. Lindsey named that "Yes, I left cookies and juice and water for those who had provided me care." Martin went back into the dwelling, and brought out the scant supplies that had been left, dropping these in Rev. Lindsey's lap, saying "In war you leave nothing, no evidence you were ever here. Except... we know, and we will remember you."

At Mareng, they waited for hours. A plane landed, describing that they were scouting for land mines from the air. The insidious nature of war is that many artillery shells had been left in the middle of roads or in places where villages had developed, without knowing these could explode at any moment and without warning. With no sign of their own charter, the pilot asked if they wanted to join their flight. While they would have saved the cost of the flight that had just been arranged, the team knew their own pilot would be flying in and arrive with no one to fly out and no one to pay for his time and fuel. So, they waited hours more until their plane came.

As Martin, Paul, Solomon and Rev. Lindsey returned on the single engine prop plane to the Lokichoggio customs, having come from Sudan, Rosemary looked forlorn. She explained that new interpretations of the rules of repatriation had come from the Government at Khartoum, declaring that Sudanese could not leave Sudan, even if their homes had become Kenya, or Congo or America. The four talked long into the night about the unfairness of this restriction, and that laws like this had been the norm in dealing with the Northern government, as well as neighboring nations. Ultimately, Rev. Lindsey gave them $200 each to pay for bus tickets and bribes for the Police and Customs officials, in order that his companions could return to their homes.

Before parting he asked Martin, "Your brother Chuiee is the Paramount Chief, your brother Daniel is the Chief of Duk Pajut, your brother Philip is a Government Official in the new Sudan, your brother Thor is General of SPLA, another brother is a Colonel in SPLA, what do you do?" Martin smiled and rubbed his bald head, then said "I am in Military Intelligence."

Rev. Lindsey traveled back to Nairobi, alone with God, he needed no other companion, and they were each finding their own way home. The companions he thought he would have going to Sudan, never joined him. Others had stepped forward, becoming good friends. Along the way, he had also come to understand this journey as an encounter with God, a struggle of faith. He recognized his quest for trust and relationships had meant being courier for dowry, letters and small packages; being courier for $3,000,000 to compensate those who had gone unpaid for years. He came bearing the name of a group of refugee lost sons, searching for their parents, and returned bearing the new name for the son of a Chief, to no longer be illegitimate; bearing the word of God to this church, and providing pastoral care to ministers who themselves were hurting and in need; providing the return of a Prodigal Son made possible by his gift; providing the means to change the cultivation practices of a people virtually in the Garden of Eden. He had come as a mainline Protestant American minister, never having had to face war, he returned home having tasted Sudan, witnessing the cost of Civil War's genocide, and having been reborn as African. He had spent everything he had brought along, and not only had this helped to change the culture, it had changed him. Conflict had been experienced firsthand in a war zone, and he would never be the same.

Arriving at Wilson Commercial Airport in Nairobi, Lindsey no longer felt like an American minister traveling through Africa or on sabbatical, he had acquired the heart of a missionary. His black clericals were smeared with sweat and the ashen, dung-dirt of Duk, his tan suit had a permanent red stain, his skin was deepened with color. He walked more deliberately, with patience and a measured step, having been a guest of honor in a foreign place. The ones who were to meet him at the airport on this end of the journey had forgotten, so after checking by phone, he sat on his backpack alone and waited for someone to be sent.

He was struck by the irony, that arriving in Africa those who were to meet him did not come, and now returning he was again alone. Yet immediately, professional people leaving the airport began asking if they could take "The Father" where he needed to go. He accepted without fear, what dangers could there be in Nairobi compared to life in Sudan? Returning to AIM Mayfield, he felt he now belonged, and there was a kinship among the missionaries on furlough.

One of the Pilots from AIM Air asked a favor of Rev. Lindsey. His eldest daughter was applying to colleges and universities in America; the international mail might not deliver her applications in a timely manner. Rev.

Lindsey was asked to hand deliver the pilot's daughter's college applications, which he added to letters from Sudanese families to their children in America.

The Sabbatical had been for him to hone skills in conflict management, as well as to envision the church, faith, ministry and life, differently. This experience in a war-zone, doing ministry without an infrastructure, had done all that. He had been an instrument of conflict resolution, helping to create new relationships, new systems and new opportunities, without a building, a budget, staff or program. He had been an instrument of God.

A mentor had described that every preacher who has ever been to Africa or to the Middle-east, afterward begins sermons with "When I stared out at the Great Nile River basin..." While he might not have to go that far, Lindsey knew he could never again tell the Parable of the Talents in in the same way, or the people living in the land of Cush, or pray about ending war, without seeing the faces of those who had endured and suffered.

When Rev. Lindsey returned to New York, he received a telephone call from a man who identified himself, "I am Panther. I am a son of Duk County." He described that he was getting married. Rev. Lindsey thought Panther was asking that he perform the wedding, when Panther described, "I have not seen his parents in over twenty years, yet the Reverend had eaten a meal with them only nights before. Would he come to their wedding, to represent Panther's family?"

Part 4

Building Mission

Eighteen months passed, as plans were authorized, funds were raised and containers loaded. A partnership was forged with Tech Serve International, a missionary-based, non-governmental organization, out of Green Brier, Arkansas. Tech Serve specializes in prefabrication of materials for shipping and assembly of buildings in undeveloped parts of the world. Imagine not having the ability to run to a local hardware or lumber for materials, imagine not being able to call for a concrete mixer delivery, imagine needing the ability to lift and set steel columns, and imagine shipping all tools, materials and medical instruments in two shipping containers to a latitude and longitude that has no roads, and you begin to understand the frustrations of this endeavor. Add to this, that ACSF represents an obscure religious non-profit tax-exempt organization with no prior record of activity providing humanitarian aid to part of a nation under United Nations Sanctions, that is now involved in yet another war (this time with Darfur).

Nine months after Rev. Lindsey's Sabbatical in Sudan, John Dau returned home for the first time in 20 years. The trip was problematic in that the number of refugees returning to Sudan had drastically escalated demand for housing, food and transportation, all along the journey. John attempted a different route, to verify that going by boat up the Nile would not be appropriate. Jim Cone's lesson that differing cultures need to explore conclusions differently provided context. In the end, it was resolved that Rev. Lindsey's initial route through Lokichoggio was the only reasonable passage and the assistance of AIM AIR was far more economical than any alternative. John's elder brother, whom Rev. Lindsey's gift had freed from problems, had become a car salesman, hotel owner and entrepreneur, who agreed to donate essential resources for logistics.

When John Dau returned to the United States in January 2006, he immediately flew to Utah for the Sundance Film Festival, where Christopher Quinn's documentary of the plight of the Lost Boys: "God Grew Tired of

Us" swept the awards, gaining instant recognition and support for John and the Clinic.

However, when John Dau returned to Central New York, this new notoriety proved yet another obstacle. One afternoon, Brandy the Catholic Social Services Social Worker for all the Sudanese Refugees in Central New York phoned Rev. Lindsey. Brandy stated that there was a rumor being passed between the Lost Boys that was quite upsetting, that "The Presbyterian Church stole money from the Lost Boys!" She was phoning Rev. Lindsey simply to inform him of this problem and hoping he might write a statement to the refugees as a letter denouncing the rumor. Rev. Lindsey said "Absolutely not!" He had learned from experience that in Dinka culture, oral debate is essential, and only when every voice could be satisfied, could there be resolution, a letter denouncing a rumor would only add to the problem. He asked that Brandy arrange a meeting as soon as possible, to listen to the complaints and try to seek common understanding. The meeting was arranged for the morning of Valentine's Day 2006 at the Catholic Social Services: Refugee Resettlement Office building.

Rev. Lindsey, Brandy and another American Social Worker all Caucasian, were greeted by a dozen Sudanese young men, then John Dau entered accompanied by three additional Sudanese men. Immediately an argument ensued, with several of the Sudanese thanking Brandy and Rev. Lindsey for coming, and demanding "Who has called this meeting, because only the President of the Lost Boys could call a meeting of the Lost Boys?" Each in turn, postured, regarding his being a Lost Boy of Duk County, and their struggle. John Dau described that he had previously been the President of the Lost Boys, but had resigned this title to work on the Clinic.

After an hour, Rev. Lindsey spoke up. "I am sorry to interrupt, but I AM the one who called this meeting. I may have had no power or authority to do so, as I am not a Lost Boy from Sudan, but, I am a son of Duk. I have been to Duk in the last year, I have lived at Duk; the earth of Duk is in me; I know personally and I care about the people of South Sudan having been welcomed into the homes of parents many of you have not seen in 20 years; but, I have been identified as a "Son of Duk". I had been instructed by your Elder Gideon, to bring Good News to the Sons of Duk that there are again Cattle at Duk. The Presbyterian Church has been a sponsor for Sudanese refugees coming to America. We have raised funds for building a clinic to serve your families at Duk Payuel. However, Brandy has told me there was a question of broken trust, that someone believed money had been stolen from the Sudanese. The Presbyterian Church would not steal from Sudanese. I am here to face this accusation, to answer this charge."

Suddenly, the leaders fractured to each explain their own fund raising appeals. Two of the Sudanese, other than John Dau, had been attempting to raise funds in Syracuse to build their own additional clinics in other villages in South Sudan, through the Catholic and Episcopal Churches, but had had very limited results. A third described that prior to creation of ACSF, John Dau had been President of the Lost Boys Education Fund, raising scholarship aid for Sudanese to attend college. Yet, since John Dau's attention had gone to the clinic, this fund had had no new donors.

Several different cultural issues were named, primary was power, influence and authority. There is what is known as The Tall Poppy Syndrome, that anything standing out in a field must be eliminated as standing out. Inter-related to this, in Dinka culture there is little personal identity, or property. If an individual receives an inheritance, this belongs to the tribe and the tribal leaders can determine how to use the windfall to benefit the tribe, regardless of the individual's wishes. The documentary film had given John Dau notoriety, and by implication because "Movie Stars" make outrageous incomes, the millions of dollars grossed by the film should be determined by the leadership of the Lost Boys. If the revenues from the film had gone to the clinic, rather than the projects the leadership might determine to fund, this was understood as theft by the church, stealing from the Sudanese refugees.

Rev. Lindsey explained that the Church had received nothing from the film, either. There are different kinds of films, and many have a script of lines to be read, with actors to play the parts, which are film that take in billions of dollars. But a documentary, is a film of life, there are no actors, no writers, and because of this, the one who directs and the one who produces the film make money for distribution of the picture, but no one else does. John Dau and the other two men who were interviewed throughout the film, had made appearances at the showing of the film which inspired people to give to the projects they represent. In America, another cultural difference is that with non-profit organizations like a Church, or Clinic or Education Fund, rather than the individual, or their leaders deciding where money should go, the one giving the money could decide, and by Law the donors wishes must be followed or the money given back.

Jack Howard, a member of the First Presbyterian Church at Skaneateles who cared affectionately for John Dau as a grandfather, became Project Manager for construction. Jack gave of himself tirelessly, as he worked 70 and 80 hours per week, every week for over three years midwifing the clinic from a concept into reality. In November 2006, two forty-foot-long steel shipping containers were loaded at Green Brier, AR. for Mombassa, Kenya. Inside were a diesel powered electric generator, steel beams and girders, construction equipment, and medical equipment, in short the entire clinic in a box. The first obstacle was shipping, as many cargo containers have been lost at sea.

Thern Sudan, where there were no paved roads. All of which needed to be accomplished, for the volunteers to arrive to clear the soil, level the site, and build the Clinic before the rainy season began anew in April and lasted for none months.

Tia: This Is Africa: Problems and Miracles

Tech Serve International, which had been a faithful partner in manufacturing and purchasing materials, then loading these into the containers, suddenly reported that they had other projects that were behind schedule, and they could not provide volunteers to supervise construction in Sudan. Don Cross and Richard Way, members of the Presbyterian Church in Skaneateles who cared passionately about this mission, traveled to Arkansas to supervise the loading of the containers. They spoke with Tech Serve construction volunteers about the Clinic at Sudan, and several became very interested. Richard Way and Don Cross were impressed by these volunteers, who worked for a stipend, and began every shift with prayer. The difficulty, that only later was discerned, was that the ACSF Board of Directors understood these volunteers were trained and supervised by Tech Serve International; while the Officers of Tech Serve International understood these individuals were independent contractors being recruited by ACSF. Consequently, these "missionaries" were unsupervised mercenaries, without direction, except that their expenses were paid to go to Sudan.

In the first week of September 2006, the containers were sealed and loaded aboard a cargo ship to travel down the Mississippi River, to the Gulf of Mexico, there to journey between Florida and Cuba and across the Atlantic. The ship then passed through the Straits of Gibraltar and across the Mediterranean Sea, down through the Suez Canal, across the Red Sea and out into the Indian Ocean, arriving at port in Mombasa, Kenya. Over the centuries thousands of containers had fallen overboard in storms and whole ships had gone down.

January 6th, 2007, the Day of Epiphany, word was received that one of the containers had been stopped at Customs in Mombassa, Kenya. The whereabouts of the second container was a mystery. ACSF wired money to a Dinka man in Nairobi, for him to take to Mombassa, in order to pay the duty on importing this container to Sudan. However, when the New York Bank processed the wire transfer, suddenly all assets of ACSF and all assets of the First Presbyterian Church at Skaneateles were frozen by the United States Government, due to sanctions against Sudan. Ten days transpired, as the Church leadership worked through channels at the State Department to recognize that the containers contained materials for building a clinic for humanitarian aid.

Finally, on the 20th of January, the container was released from Port and allowed to be transported by truck to Duk Payuel. About this time, it was discerned that Container Two had been hijacked at Port, loaded aboard a train and sent to Lokichoggio, Kenya, where it was being held for additional "Customs duties" (ransom). Who had authorized this train shipment or why, was never made clear. However, once the duty was paid, the container was released. The transporters tried to insist upon shipping the container back to Mombassa, for an additional fee; however, it was eventually agreed that while container one had been sent along the traditional route through Uganda, to then travel to Duk Payuel, this container would drive across the open Savannah from Loki to Duk. Whether either semi-tractor trailer could travel fully loaded on sand without becoming stuck, finding their way along migratory paths to this remote village in the bush, identified only by latitude and longitude coordinates, was unknown? Whether either container had been opened or damaged in transit was also unknown, as was how long transit would take?

Recognizing that the rainy season would arrive whether the containers did or not, ACSF prepared a schedule for volunteers to travel to Sudan. Don Cross, Ted Kinder and Mark Dewitt all of Skaneateles, New York were considered

Team One, who left New York on February 12, 2007, two years after the first meeting of ACSF with Dr. David Bowman. Rather than contracting around a table in a Boardroom, relationship building and resource development had taken two years, but it was taking place. February 14th, Syracuse was hit with a record snow storm that blanketed the east coast. Had they left 72 hours later, Team One would not have could leave the United States for a week, but as it was, they made all their connections, as did their luggage, arriving at Duk Payuel on February 14th.

When the AIM/AIR plane was unloaded, the three exhausted Presbyterians from Skaneateles were led into a long dark building, crowded with people. Each later described having a sinking feeling that perhaps the Dinka were cannibals and they were being led to their own sacrifice. But as their eyes adjusted to the darkness, they recognized Rev. Peter and Rev. Paul, Chief Daniel Deng Leek and Paramount Chief Chuiee Deng Leek, all from Rev. Lindsey's photos. They introduced themselves as friends of Rev. Lindsey who had come to fulfill the promise, by building the clinic. They were given a hero's welcome, as proclamation was translated to the assembled village, that these men had come from Rev. Lindsey to work with the village in building their clinic. A fatted calf was slaughtered and a great feast took place. The three suddenly recognized the very real level of desperation among this people, when during dinner, they had finished their meals and children then began gnawing on the bones and licking the plates they had already eaten off, to have any left-over scrap or grease.

Thursday morning, February 15th, the American contractors began stretching level lines and marking corner posts. While they worked with all the skills and expertise learned in years in the trades, wild brushfires would begin to blaze behind and all around them. The Sudanese explained that theirs is a cattle dependent culture, and the cattle eat only the tender young shoots, not the razor-sharp grasses that have grown six and eight feet tall, so in this season the people light fires that burn the tall grasses. It was disconcerting to realize that behind you was a wall of flame twelve feet high and half a mile long, but burning in the opposite direction. All through the night, the horizon would be illuminated as the embers of fires often reignited by spontaneous combustion. In addition to the grass fires, used for clearing the land, being a cattle culture there were massive quantities of dung, that once dried was collected and burned. The ash from these dung fires was rubbed on the skin to keep flies from biting. But the smell of smoke and particularly from the dung fires was so constant as to become noxious. Clearing the ground with fire, also chased small animals and vermin from the area, for building.

Shipping Containers and Volunteer Contractors

There are times when God shows off, like hardening the heart of Pharaoh with 10 plagues before parting the Red Sea. February 15th, about 11pm, Don saw something large moving slowly towards their camp. He thought it was an elephant, or some other African beast, but then he saw the word GREENLEAF on the side, recognizing this as one of the two containers.

Shipped fourteen weeks before, lost on a truck for nearly two weeks on the African Savannah, the container arrived within 30 hours of the volunteers, shortly after the exact location for construction had been identified. He returned to his tent and opened his Bible, which fell open to Psalm 138.

Psalm 138 Of David.

1 I will praise you, O LORD, with all my heart; before the "gods" I will sing your praise.

2 I will bow down toward your holy temple and will praise your name for your love and your faithfulness, for you have exalted above all things your name and your word.

3 When I called, you answered me; you made me bold and stouthearted.

4 May all the kings of the earth praise you, O LORD, when they hear the words of your mouth.

5 May they sing of the ways of the LORD, for the glory of the LORD is great.

6 Though the LORD is on high, he looks upon the lowly, but the proud he knows from afar.

7 Though I walk in the midst of trouble, you preserve my life; you stretch out your hand against the anger of my foes, with your right hand you save me.

8 The LORD will fulfill his purpose for me; your love, O LORD, endures forever— do not abandon the works of your hands.

Friday the 16th, Don, Ted and Mark began working with volunteers to unload the container. At port, the loaded steel container had been picked off the deck of the ship and placed atop the tractor trailer with a crane, but in the bush, there were no crane lifts. Everything except the steel beams and generator were unloaded by hand. Using jacks, they attempted to lift the container, but the heat and sand and weight had seized the container to the trailers pins, and two jacks were broken in the process. Finally, the container was worked loose on the pins, chains were connected from the container to nearby trees, and like a cartoon from the Roadrunner and Coyote, the truck drove out from under the container, which landed on the ground with a crash. The following morning, the second container was parked outside the work site, and more quickly than the first, unloaded. The containers had never been opened, everything loaded was delivered. However, the heat and dropping of the container had done damage to the generator. Undaunted, Don Cross set about rewiring the generator, bypassing a pressure relief valve like a cardiac surgeon bypassing clogged arteries.

On Sunday, they worshiped God with the Village, with Don Cross providing the second sermon. Sunday night, the youngest boy in the village flipped a switch and for the first time in their lives saw the power of electricity as the Clinic was illuminated with electric light. Then it was the youngest girl's turn, as power lit the village of mud huts. The youngest children had been selected, so that years from now, when they were aged, they would be able to remember and recount for others how they had turned on the power for their village.

While Don had been working on the electric generator, a well repairman had been "fixing" the only water well that stood in the village. Monday, the repairman became angry and walked off the job. Trying to determine how to proceed they tied a rock to a rope and dropped this into the well, expecting to hear a splash. Instead they heard a dry clatter, as the rock hit other rocks at the bottom of the well, with only inches of water. They went to the Duk County Commissioner, explaining the need for water, not only for the Village, and for the clinic, but for making concrete. The Commissioner threw up his hands, asking if they thought he were God to make water appear from rock? That evening they went to a wedding in the village, and it happened that in the dark of night at that wedding, a California Well Driller named Alan Pike walked up to them, describing that he had been sent by his Church to drill wells as a mission in 1991, and he had never returned to America. On Tuesday, the Well Driller began boring a new hole in the ground, when connections were made to the generator, by nightfall the clinic site had a pressurized well, that water was available at the turn of a spigot, rather than pumping, or submerging a bucket in a stagnant pool. These were dramatic developments in the first few days, that everyone, not least of which the three Americans gave thanks to God for witnessing.

In the days that followed, Team One built frames and mixed concrete in their own electric powered cement mixer, for the pouring of footers. The concrete had to be wet down and covered with plastic to preserve it from curing too quickly in the 120-degree heat. Then came the task of setting steel columns and trusses, complicated because the steel as well as the air was 120 degrees, and because no one knew how the trusses were supposed to be assembled.

Following the carpenter's rules of plumb, level and square, they learned by doing.

March 3rd, the plane arrived to deliver Team Two: Jim, Jack, Brad, Michael and Grant, and to return Ted Kinder and Mark Dewitt to Nairobi for site-seeing in Africa before returning to the States. Moments after the plane left the ground, a neighboring tribe, the Murle, attacked the Village. The Dinka people are a tribe raising cattle and goats. The Murle are a tribe that have survived for centuries by poaching and stealing from neighboring tribes.

The Murle, predominantly are infertile due to sexually transmitted diseases, who procreate through the kidnapping of children. For weeks, the contractors had seen the Murle, like predators, assessing and investigating the site, searching for opportunity to steal cattle and children. Villagers had routinely chased them away, and shot stray gunfire in the air when the Murle were in the area.

When Attacked, Are You a Missionary or A Mercenary?

On March 3rd, the Murle tribe attacked. First indication had been that a woman came to the site of where the clinic was being built with a cut on her hand. They bandaged her hand, thinking little of it, until another person and another were brought to the clinic, and they began to recognize gunshot wounds. One man was shot in the thigh and bleeding profusely. Michael, who was a registered Nurse as well as a carpenter, and Don Cross who was an EMT with the Skaneateles Volunteer Fire Department, applied constant pressure to the wound, kept the man hydrated and attempted to keep him from going into shock. The volunteers put their own lives at risk nursing the wounded. They transported this wounded man in the back of a small pickup truck to a doctor 45 miles away. Quite literally, they saved this man's life. Three days later, this wounded man was back working at the clinic job site, describing to others how the clinic had saved him. Several others were not as fortunate and died immediately from wounds sustained. In total 45 cows were stolen, 7 people were wounded and 3 persons were killed.

As horrific as this scene was, nothing could compare with the greater abuses that followed. A church in Virginia had donated to the clinic, then offered one of their young men as a volunteer. In panic and fear at what had taken place, this young man began taking photos of the wounded and the dead. Crew Foreman, Jim, a devout evangelical, posted these photos on his website, along with his assumptions that "these heathens were not even given a Christian burial". Several of the photos portrayed "the Great White Hunter Jim, heroically riding in a jeep to chase the evil natives." These photos posted on his own website, Jim used to fundraise for his "ministry". Others showed Jim posing with golf clubs, making the center of the Village his personal driving range, still others showed a malnourished child attempting to eat one of Jim's golf balls. Several showed the bodies of the dead, disfigured by bullets. In the worst sense of the word, these Americans violated the morals and ethics and integrity of what the clinic embodied. Where the Presbyterian volunteers from Skaneateles had been careful to honor the local people, to faithfully attend worship at the local Anglican Church, to listen to and respect their faith stories; Jim's team believed themselves to be morally superior and righteous, therefore enabling themselves to treat the Sudanese people as less than human. While Jim's crew began every work session in private prayer and Bible study, they ignored the Christian faith of the community they were serving. When Sudanese refugees in America learned of these abuses, they challenged the ACSF Board for these horrific actions. ACSF immediately fired Jim, demanding he take down the photos and website, as well as requiring he write a letter of apology to be shared with the Dinka people. While pleading sadness that this had taken place, he never followed through on the simple requirement of an apology requesting forgiveness.

Bags of dry cement for the clinic were trucked from Juba. One of the tools in the shipping containers had been a motorized cement mixer, that could hold two bags of cement at a time. This was combined with water, sand and aggregate. Sand was plentiful at Duk Payuel, clean and fine. Aggregate was more problematic in that there was no granite, marble or quartz. The only aggregate available was volcanic residue, that was extremely porous and hard. "Skridding" this was difficult because the volcanic rock would gouge large tracks through the cement. Tech Serve had created a mold for manufacturing concrete block, however local Ethiopian masons were found who had experience making bricks and laying these up in concrete walls. The mortar joints were thick, and afterwards the walls all needed to be parged with additional concrete, but they were plumb and level and square. Steel doors and frames had been shipped, due to concern for termites as well as clinic security. Continually the American supervisors had to remind the Ethiopian masons that door openings needed to include space for the steel frame, as wood doors could always be shortened or narrowed dependent upon the opening, but not steel. One afternoon GG, the senior Ethiopian mason left the job site and became so drunk as to stay away from the clinic site for six days. Alcoholism and depression are realities after +20 years of living with war.

The 72-Year-Old to The Rescue

Chuck Williams was a 72-year-old retired educator, and a member of First Presbyterian Church. When the call went out for volunteers, Chuck was among the first to respond. For the twenty years prior to his retirement, Mr. Williams had been responsible for publishing the New York State Regents' Exam. Several scoffed and worried about this academic publisher, but Chuck was undeterred. The two factors most did not know, were that Chuck and his wife annually traveled to Central America for excursions and were naturally accustomed to high heat and humidity; and Chuck Williams' undergraduate education had been as a chemical engineer, specifically writing his Senior Thesis at Alma College on Principles of Concrete. No selection of a volunteer could have been better, as Chuck could test the tensile strength of the lava aggregate, determining how large of sections of flooring could be poured at a time. In addition, despite his age, and willingness to eat anything and everything he was served, Mr. Williams was the one member out of all the American volunteers who never became ill.

As Chuck Williams prepared to fly home, Don Cross and Mark DeWitt volunteered to make a return trip to work for an additional two weeks supervising construction, teaching the Sudanese the finish carpentry of hanging cabinets and basic electrical wiring. On May 1st, the Medical Staff recruited from across Kenya and Uganda boarded a charter at Lokichoggio to begin operations at the Duk Lost Boys Clinic.

Part 5

Developing Mission

June 1st, the Moderator of the General Assembly of the Presbyterian Church (USA) visited the Presbytery of Cayuga-Syracuse and learned of First Presbyterian Church's mission commitments in South Sudan. Over dinner, they discussed ecumenism and the possibility for diversity within the Presbyterian Church (Conservative and Liberal), when the Moderator tried to make a point about the authority of the Orthodoxy by describing "But, do you not believe it is important that we identify ourselves as Presbyterians, saved in the name of Jesus?" It was a statement she had surely repeated over and over in the wars for control of the Church. However, this was Trinity Sunday weekend. Rev. Lindsey thought a moment and responded deliberately, "The Church I serve has been in partnership with a people, a people who have known God since before the time of the Babylonian Exile, a people who have only learned the name of Jesus within the last forty years and for which they have paid with genocide. I know Jesus to have been the historic embodiment of God saving the world. I know our faith to be real in ways I never imagined, which I can only attribute to the power of the Holy Spirit among us. So, I believe there is a distinction needed in our language between *Jesus* and the *Holy Spirit*. I have had to struggle, to forgive those who went to this Village at our request, professing that they were Missionaries of Jesus, who took golf clubs to Sudan, who refused to worship in the community's Church, and who acted as mercenaries. I also know that when I personally was near death, sleeping on the bloodied sands of war-ravaged South Sudan, a non-seminary trained Anglican priest prayed by my bedside all night long. A priest who never went beyond high school. My dearest friend is the grandson of the Tribal Witch-doctors who personally is responsible for conversion of this tribe to a variety of Christian faiths. Am I to tell these believers, our covenant partners in doing mission, that their ancestors, whose dust is now in my life, their ancestors could not be "saved" because those ancestors did not know "Jesus" who is our personification of God's love? Or are we to work together to change the world and pray for each other to

Almighty God, as Jesus did, to the God whom some call YHWH, others El Shaddai, others Elohim, and still others call Allah?"

Telecommunications

Six weeks after the clinic began operation, Rev. Lindsey's telephone rang. His brother-in-law, George Giatzoglou, an executive at INTELSAT Communications Corporation out of Washington, DC stated, "We have been following your work in Southern Sudan and would like to make the following corporate donation. We will give you the names and contacts for distributors out of Nairobi, Kenya. You negotiate the best deal possible, whereupon we will cut a check for the cost of installing a Satellite dish and three years of service for High Speed Internet Communications." Suddenly, here was the possibility of reliable communication. The staff would not be isolated, if they encountered tribal warfare, civil war, a case beyond their capabilities, they would not be alone.

On June 28th word reached America that the first baby, having had prenatal care, had been born at the Duk Lost Boys Clinic. The male baby, born at the Duk Lost Boys Clinic at the Village of Duk Payuel, in Duk County, was appropriately named "Duk". A month later when the second baby was born, he was named "Duk 2". In Dinka culture, "Deng" is a very common name meaning "It was raining when the baby was born". Now, a new name had been added to the culture, to be named "Duk" meant born with pre-natal care at Duk Lost Boys Clinic.

Among the women presenting for Prenatal Care, Dr. Miriam quickly diagnosed one woman would be requiring a Cesarean Section, which the Clinic could not handle. Six weeks prior, mother and baby would have died due to complications of delivery. Instead, the Clinic could contract for her family to pay AIM AIR and a nurse from the Clinic to fly to Lokichoggio, where she could give birth in a hospital. In the month of August, a woman gave birth to her child at her home (hut) at Pok Tap. There were complications, so the mother wrapped up her baby and walked through 20 inches of standing water 18 miles to the Clinic at Duk Payuel. Upon examination, Dr. Miriam diagnosed that mother and baby both had malaria, and the mother was extremely anemic having lost a great deal of blood postpartum. They had medications for malaria, but had no medications left for anemia. The Medical staff bartered with a villager at Duk Payuel, who sacrificed a goat, and the woman was given the iron rich goat liver to eat. She remained at the clinic growing in strength for 24 hours, whereupon she left. The staff heard nothing of the woman for two weeks, uncertain if she had made it back home or died along the way. One day, she again walked into the clinic, carrying her baby, both strong and healthy. She had walked the 18 miles home, rested, nursed and cared for her child until they were strong enough, and she had walked back for her baby's physical by the doctor.

The First John Dau Sudan Foundation

During the summer of 2007 John Dau left Direct Change to create a new foundation. A foundation that would provide he and his family in America a steady income, to develop his skills as a fundraiser, balancing funding the Clinic at Duk Payuel with the construction of five additional new clinics in South Sudan. John worked with philanthropists he had met in Park City, Utah at the Sundance Film Festival to register and incorporate the John Dau Sudan Foundation. Problems began as the existing clinic ran out of reserve funding, yet there were constant assurances that the existent clinic would continue to be funded, while JDSF pledged funds for the construction of additional clinics.

September 5th, 2007 JDSF held its first fundraising event and JDSF received a pledge of $250,000 for the building of a second clinic. Additional questions arose concerning the division of responsibilities and creation of a business plan for the transition from ACSF to JDSF. Part of JDSF's goal became providing International Medical Mission trips including partnering with an Ophthalmology program out of Nepal. Yet, ACSF's standing commitment had been to provide health care according to the standards of the World Health Organization (WHO) guidelines, not opportunities for "Medical Tourism". An on-going question for the Clinic has been the balance of operational funding over against the more exciting creation of additional new programs. The American Care for Sudan Foundation Board struggled with whether the clinic was being abandoned, or whether their control of their program was being taken away. This was not a clear or easy transition, but more a matter of discernment. Almost immediately there were problems between John Dau and the John Dau Sudan Foundation "philanthropists". The tension was not only over control, and direction of funding the Duk Clinic versus creating clinics named for the donors; these JDSF Board/philanthropists had anticipated a financial return on their investment, despite this being a non-profit corporation, and there was no money for dividends.

Medical Mission Trips, Not Medical Tourism

Dan Friedman a Medical Student at Cornell University (NYC) became a Summer Intern with Dr. Barbara Connor for 2007. Dan greatly assisted ACSF by making connections with UNICEF and IMF, MEDS, as well as the Sudanese Embassy. Labor Day weekend 2007, Rev. Dr. Lindsey was contacted by Glenn Geelhoed MD, on the faculty of the Departments of Surgery, International Medicine and (Microbiology) Infectious Diseases at George Washington University: Medical College for a face to face meeting at Syracuse University Medical School, concerning Medical Missions. This led to an invitation to Rev. Lindsey to address George Washington University: Medical College in late September, and their sharing a meeting with the Sudanese Ambassador on September 25th 2007. Rev. Dr. Lindsey's understanding being that Dr. Geelhoed desired to lead an international medical mission trip of Medical Students to the clinic in South Sudan, December 26, 2007 - January 15, 2008.

In early December 2007, Rev. Dr. Lindsey established relationships with Presbyteries across the United States concerned about the Sudan, through the Sudan Mission Network meeting at Louisville, KY. While at this conference of missionaries and those concerned with the Sudan, Dr. Geelhoed phoned to suggest that Rev. Lindsey not only participate in the first Medical mission trip to Duk Clinic, but share in leadership of the Medical mission to the Clinic at Duk Payuel, less than four weeks in the future.

The December 2007 - January 2008 Medical Mission Team represented a diversity of interests: Dr. Glenn Geelhoed and Rev. Craig Lindsey, Dennis a retired Government Statistician who had become a professional photographer, John a first year Medical Student from India, Kristie an Infectious Disease student working at NIH, Christy a Public Health Student, Denise a Rwandan refugee planning to begin Medical School, Marshall a licensed chiropractor who had previously served as a trauma nurse, and Bethany a 16 year old High School student from Wisconsin who dreamed of a career in Medicine in a 3rd world country. There was to have been an additional student, a 3rd year Surgical resident, but as the team waited at the airport she phoned to say she could not come because her sister-in-law was dying on hospice care. Complicating matters, insofar as she was the Surgical Resident, she had been responsible for carrying the only anesthesia available for this Medical Mission at the Clinic.

Flying into A Warzone to Get to Sudan

During a layover in London, Denny, the 70-year-old photographer, became separated from the group. Despite searching Heathrow Airport, he could not be found. Their flight was delayed because of a bad tire on the landing gear. The group began to be filled with fears that none would make it to Duk Payuel and return; and even if they did, what could be done without anesthesia? Rev. Lindsey moved into "MOM-mode" making certain everyone kept track of their belongings and stayed within sight of one another, while he kept sight of each, and contacted the police with a missing person's report. Several planes to Nairobi had been cancelled, so every ticket was accounted for. Denny eventually made it back to the airport, and discovering the plane was full, attempted to purchase a ticket for the next available flight, doing so alerted police to his whereabouts. Denny was summarily brought to the group under Police guard, looking very frustrated and sheepish. Just as boarding was announced, CNN broadcast that in the

Kenyan National election, the President of Kenya, who had lost five of the seven provinces of Kenya, had declared himself to have won re-election, then immediately closed all petrol (gasoline) stations, and was shutting down radio and television broadcast during a state of Martial-law. Rev. Lindsey reflected on the change from traveling solo and arriving in Nairobi to discover he had no support, to this time arriving in Kenya during Civil War. Dr. David Bowman's warning "TIA = This Is Africa" not only related to a different culture, a tribal culture, where containers are hijacked and wells run dry, but where civil war is a very real possibility in any country.

The commercial carrier flew to Nairobi's Kenyatta International Airport and was the very last commercial plane to arrive in the country. The group gathered bags and made their way through customs, where Dr. Geelhoed had already commandeered a group of taxis and negotiated the price in Swahili, to transport the nine passengers and luggage across the city of Nairobi to the private charter airstrip at Wilson Air Field used by AIM/AIR. Rev. Lindsey suddenly oversaw paying the carriers what Dr. Geelhoed negotiated. He recalled how previously Sudanese had been spending his money, and now Dr. Geelhoed was doing so. Driving through Nairobi was an anxious trip as several roads and intersections were closed by rioting, piles of tires were assembled and ignited a fire, while men with AK47s shot into the air.

Arriving at the AIM/AIR strip of Wilson airfield the pilot had already put the plane away, fearing the group had been unable to arrive in country. Simultaneously, the President's orders had made fuel for the flight to Sudan limited. Rev. Lindsey recognized the pilot as the same one he had met years before at AIM Mayfield and Lindsey had carried his daughter's college applications to America for mailing. Under duress, the team were able to convince the pilot to fly the group to El Dorset, where the plane could be refueled, and could make Loki before nightfall. AIM/AIR use small single engine propeller planes without instrumentation for night flying, so pilots need to land before nightfall. Being a Missionary corporation, the pilots pray before flying. Flying into El Doret, there were bursts of gunfire, and the pilot described that Dinka and Nuer had barricaded families of each other's tribe inside Churches, then lit the Churches afire.

(Nairobi in flames and rioting, December 31, 2007)

As the Churches were burning, people inside tried to escape, and doing so, those outside made a game of shooting them to death. As the plane took off, fires were seen burning, while groups of women and children were hiding behind hills and buildings. The pilot shook his head saying there was nothing we could do; people were being herded for killing.

The plane arrived at Lokichoggio on New Year's Eve, but any celebratory mood was extinguished by the pall of what was happening across the Nation of Kenya. Kenya had been so tranquil and peaceful for decades, while South Africa, Uganda, Ethiopia, Sudan and the Democratic Republic of Congo were each in conflict. The world had taken for granted that civil war and rioting could not occur in Kenya, but just as September 11th in America, security and safety, all trusts and relationships, even humanity itself were violated, as all old tribal animosities were played out, with one family raping and murdering a neighbor family, simply for being alive in the same place and not the same.

Lokichoggio was different than it had been in 2005. At that time (April 2005), Loki had been an active trade depot, with enormous goliath planes taxiing in and out as the United Nations delivered essential food and supplies to multiple African nations at war, soldiers of differing nations and peacekeepers of the United Nations had been everywhere. Now the sides of the airstrip were littered with the decaying skeletons of these great heavier-than-air planes. An old male lion lay sunning himself at the far end of the airstrip. The AIM/AIR Hostel had become a campus with motel style cabins, bar, television, a pool table, as well as tents with electric lights and hot and cold running water.

Early the next morning, January 01, 2008 a fresh pilot had gassed up the plane and was prepared to fly the first visiting Medical Mission team to Duk Payuel. Arriving at Duk was surreal, all the landmarks were still present, the abandoned water tower of the British, the three Palm trees that had been an altar for the Tribal Witch Doctor's sacrifices, but where there had been one couple living here, now there were an estimated 1700 people, John Dau and Dr. Miriam waiting for us. Quickly backpacks and medical equipment duffel bags were carried away, as the team listened to the singing of the Village and paraded up to the Church. Different from the Church at Pok Tap which had been steel with a high roof and a wall only at the Chancel end, the Church at Duk Payuel was an enormous thatched roof hut 75 feet long, with small windows to allow the air and small amounts of light to filter in. This was as dark, cool and shadowed as the other had been bright, arid and hot. Following prayers of thanksgiving to Almighty God for safe travel, and speeches of welcome, we walked to the Clinic site, on the way passing the abandoned Water tank.

Duk Payuel is a flat landscape without a single hill for miles, there is a watering hole, and many small scrub trees, as well as great immense ghost trees. The ghost trees were hard wood trees planted by the missionaries in the 1920s, which had grown 60 and 75 feet tall, ten feet across. But one of the strange natural relationships of Africa, the birds consume seeds of vine plants, then nest in these trees. When the birds defecate, the seeds attach to the high branches of the trees, as the seeds germinate, the vines grow from the branches to the ground where they take root, creating a perimeter around the trunk of the tree hiding the tree from sunlight and moisture.

Eventually, all that remains are the 75-foot-long root-vines hanging from branches supported by the withered stalk of what were mighty trees. Everywhere there are cows and people, an estimated 3,500,000 cows, yet like the people, these were malnourished, diseased, infested with worms in their bellies and intestinal tracks, without enough water in the dry season to produce milk. Suddenly, the origins of the word disease became real, as the people and cattle were not listless, nor did they act with intention and motivation, all were dis-eased, agitated, unsure, motivated by fear, or immediate gratification, unable to consider long-term effects.

In the midst of the crowd stood John Dau smiling, delighted to be responsible for bringing medicine to his village and people. John had arrived weeks before with another of the Lost Boys, who desired to give to his village a school and orphanage. The Utah based John Dau Sudan Foundation had imploded in hostilities and John had returned to Sudan. John Dau led the Medical Mission team from the Church to the Clinic compound. John described arriving to find that the Clinic had been filthy dirty, as the staff and village accustomed to dirt floors and mud huts did not comprehend the idea of sterile cleanliness, so they had instructed the staff to wash down cobwebs and wash out the dirt. Throughout the next several weeks' cleanliness, authority and ownership of the Clinic would be a continual problem.

Seeing the Clinic for the first time, Rev. Lindsey openly wept, in awe and thanksgiving. Here was the dream he had described to the Village three years prior, realized. As community leaders had described having been repeatedly lied to and betrayed by their own government and by strangers from foreign lands, this Clinic with not only building but staff and medicines was a physical manifestation that their promise had been fulfilled. Even more, that a people who had only ever known poverty, war, oppression and disease, would by the fulfillment of this promise have opportunity; opportunities for health and strength and peace, the true difference between poverty and riches.

Dr. Geelhoed shook his head and described, "Emperors and Kings, Governments and Corporations have built palaces adorned in gold and fountains. But a Church, in Central New York, nearly all of whom will never see this themselves, have built a place of healing and care and compassion! Now, we are to build capacity." Water, Electricity, and a Clinic Building had been created, equipment, medicines and staff supplied. Capacity building would involve installation and use of Internet Communication, Consistent Record Keeping, additional Training of Staff, developing possibilities for

Surgery, Housing for Staff, fencing to control the compound, International Medical Assistance certification of World Health Organization standards.

There was still much to do in construction and cleaning, as there was no ceiling, electric light fixtures were dangling at odd angles, and several of the observation rooms were filled with debris, empty oil drums, cardboard boxes, garbage and ladders. Scorpions and snakes had taken up residence amid the refuse. In small groups the members of the Medical Mission Team walked throughout the village, taking in elements of the culture, picking up on pre-existent medical conditions, and representing the clinic to the population. Among those whom the team met was the SPLA Commandant. He expressed great gratitude in Americans coming to provide aid. He expressed concern that the Murle had recently attacked villagers to kidnap children, so he would post sentries to protect the mission team while they slept.

As the evening waned, John Dau and Rev. Lindsey sat together beneath the stars. Lindsey recalled looking up at these stars the night before leaving three years before. Again, he was amazed by their brilliance. John Dau described that in Dinka culture there are constellations of stars. Ancestors of great valor and courage had become guardians from the heavens, who held the leash of dogs and cows composed of stars. The two compared constellations from their ancestors.

John Dau described that the clinic and the staff needed many things, and because this Medical Mission Team had arrived without anesthesia, this was something else the clinic needed. The staff needed vegetables and fruits. The clinic needed tools and materials. He and his companions would go to buy what was needed, but they needed money to do so. Rev. Lindsey, Dr. Geelhoed and each of the students went through their own reserves of cash to find as many newer, larger bills as possible. In total, they raised $3,500 from the Mission Team's own assets. John Dau took this, pledging to return within the week, to celebrate the formal dedication of the clinic and reimburse this money. The following morning John Dau and his companions were gone. Throughout the next two weeks, John Dau would occasionally call by phone to provide assurances, but did not return. Lindsey remembered how earlier he had given $3,000 to create a cultivation program, which at the time was an enormous amount of money, yet he had no evidence it had ever begun, and now they had given $3,500 that had disappeared.

The Medical Mission team assembled in the clinic at 8am. Dr. Geelhoed paired up members of the mission team and assigned each pair a member of the clinic staff. Christy and Denise worked with Cara the Midwife in OB/GYN. Kristie worked in the Lab with microbiology diagnosis. Bethany worked with Miriam the Clinical Officer. John and Marshall worked with one nurse named Paul, in infant dehydration. Craig Lindsey worked with the other nurse Johnson, in general medicine. Dr. Geelhoed and Denny the Photographer floated, to be available to all as needed. From 8 am until 1pm the team saw patients and made diagnoses. The Americans were treated as full medical doctors, asking symptoms, making examinations, diagnoses and writing prescriptions. The Clinic staff supervised and assisted in the learning of each specialty. From 1pm until 2pm the clinic and mission team shared lunch of rice and luke warm water, during which each was asked their most interesting case. At 2pm the staff and team went back to work, continuing until 6 or 7pm.

Medical Conditions and Cultural Implications

Over dinner, Dr. Geelhoed held grand rounds as each presented their day, as Dr. Geelhoed interpreted the medical conditions and the cultural implications.

Immediate lessons learned...

> • Crisis Management recognizes a group's desire to respond and act; but the impoverished may have other priorities, and donors yet a third priority set.

> • 95% of Western Health Care is expended for persons in the last 5% of life.

• 47% of Sub-Saharan population exist on less than $1 per day, which is universally true for this population.

• There is a distinction between "mortality" and "morbidity". Worldwide the primary causes of Mortality are identified by the acronym DAMMM

- Dehydration and Diarrhea

- Anaphylactic Pneumonia

- Malaria

- Measles

- Malnutrition

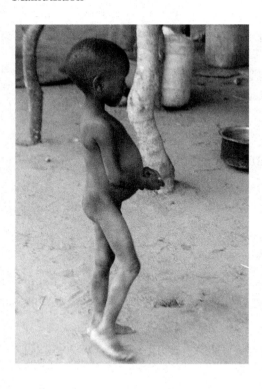

• In the cultural development from hunter/gatherers to agrarian lifestyle, hunter/gatherers operated based on "favors", while agrarian culture operated based on "debt". Favors are based on trust and relationships. Debt is financially based.

• AIDS/HIV in Africa is a short death.

• STDs: Sexually Transmitted Diseases dramatically affect fertility, meaning that an STD often prevents pregnancy. In a polygamous culture, with strict religious codes, pregnancy is vital and sexually transmitted diseases are extremely important. There is a difference between STDs which are acquired, versus infertility from birth. Imagine the correlations to the Genesis stories of Sarah, Rebecca, Rachel, Leah and Hannah! What a painful irony, to try to equate these Mothering images of Holy Scripture, overcoming barrenness to confronting STDs. Obviously, this would preach differently in the Dinka culture of Sudan than in the suburban Northeast or Midwestern United States of America.

• Heart Disease, High Blood Pressure, Obesity, Appendicitis, Hypertension are maladies of affluent society and unheard of in this population.

• Judgement comes from experience, yet experience comes from bad judgement.

• Arthritis and body aches are common due to the responsibilities of this lifestyle. Distinction between Osteo-Arthritis and Rheumatoid-Arthritis, Osteo is Large Joint related, pain usually worse in the morning, dissipating with movement throughout the day; Rheumatoid is small joint afflicted, increasingly painful throughout after activity.

• The major problem of the world is priorities. Not a question of theoretical possibilities, but what donors are willing to contribute to create.

- The development of Non-Governmental Organizations (NGOs) requires transitions from advocacy to administration to ownership to institutionalization.

- Tuberculosis is caused by a cut from sharp edged reed, which in the human body becomes a virus that is aspirated.

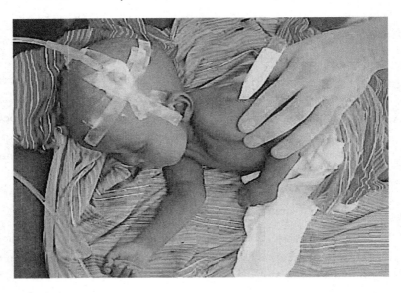

The first morning on the Pediatric unit there were several high moments, as mothers brought dehydrated, malnourished infants, and the nurse demonstrated how to place an intravenous tube directly into the veins in the head, and with rehydration children were restored to life in their mothers' arms. Yet, that afternoon, that very miracle turned to tragedy, as a mother stood in line with her infant. The child had had pneumonia, which led to dehydration. The mother had been one of those attacked and beaten the week prior by the Murle tribe, so mother and child had stayed in hiding to protect her child from being stolen, rather than seeking immediate medical attention. The child was quiet and lethargic in her mother's arms. Despite the most heroic efforts, the child was already dead. Once death was pronounced, the scene changed instantly and dramatically, from concern to mourning. The mother and grandmother who had come holding the baby, suddenly could not touch the body. Death being acknowledged, they wailed and fell to the floor, then left the body at the clinic as they sought a male head of household who was the only one who could transport the dead without being profaned.

"Maternal wastage" is a reality in this culture, as one to two years of birthing is lost in the death of a child. Birth dates and years of age are a foreign concept, that is not understood here. Making cultural adaptations, the Medical mission team learned to ask how many pregnancies a woman has had, estimating that she was married at age 15, and with nursing each pregnancy allows the body a spacing of two years. Therefore, a woman who has had nine pregnancies, would be 33-35 years of age. But the other half of the story was to ask, "And how many live children do you have?" and the woman would respond matter of fact: "two" meaning that she had buried seven of her children from miscarriage or infant death before age five years.

Morbidity in this culture includes Blindness, Deafness, Sterility, Amputation of limbs, but morbidity is not mortality, though often a circumstance leading to death.

In comparison to Western cultures, the regular diet in South Sudan has a lack of Calcium that can result in contracted muscles, like a Velossa Raptor; and lack of Iodine resulting in a goiter and related problems of the thyroid. Several women had bright red hair, which is an indication of being malnourished. Rochidic Rosary is a form of Rickets arising from a lack of Vitamin D, manifesting in markings that appear like a Catholic Rosary around the neck and upper chest.

Hook Worm, Moses' Wilderness Serpent and The A.M.A.

Another natural medical malady in this region is hook work, Giardia Protozoa, which is a microscopic parasite transmitted to humans from cow manure, that becomes water-borne during the rainy season. The hook-worm is absorbed through the palms of hands or soles of feet, or scalp. Immediate symptoms include gray foul-smelling, floating feces. The worm grows in the human blood stream, eventually blocking an artery, resulting in loss of a limb, or death. The difficulty of treatment is that if a person tries to cut out the worm, it often breaks off and re-grows. Instead, like the Biblical story of Deuteronomy and Numbers, a sharp point is inserted into the vein, piercing the worm, then slowly the point is twisted, one turn per day, wrapping the worm until the point is retracted and the whole worm extracted. In addition, this becomes the winged symbol of medicine. Yet another common malady are the parasites which infect the eyes and nose mucous, implanted by flies. The parasites cause the eyelashes to roll inward rather than out, which scratch and scar the eyes resulting in blindness. A distinction here between Infestation and Infection. While Flies cause an infection that multiplies to billions; Worms are an infestation recognizing that the worm grows to maturity but cannot reproduce within the human bloodstream.

January 5th the Team visited the County Commissioner. On the walls were a description of the circumstance of "disadvantaged groups across Duk County". At this point, the resident population of Duk Payuel was 3700 persons, among which were:

Widowed Women	533
Orphaned Children	2107
Wounded Veterans	106
Blind	36
Deaf	10
Aged	25

Elijah Becomes Elisha

On the trip back to Duk Payuel from Pok Tap, the lorries stopped at a small village. The driver introduced a man named Elijah describing that this is the Rural Deacon responsible for Rev. Lindsey's oxen and plow cultivation program. Rev. Lindsey appeared bewildered as this was not the Rural Deacon Elijah, whom he had known. Elijah smiled and explained, "Reverend, the

Original Rural Deacon: Elijah at left, wearing pink shirt; and New Rural Deacon: Elisha, at right, in Dashiki.

Rural Deacon found the work to be too difficult, so he found me and made me the Rural Deacon changing my name to Elisha, saying one day you would return to see our trust." Rev. Lindsey laughed, recognizing fulfillment of both the Parable of the Talents, and the Old Testament story of the Prophet Elijah, who had left the Mountain with the still small voice, having been told to anoint Kings and Priests, then finally to appoint his successor, and immediately Elijah had found Elisha to continue what he felt was too much for him alone.

Sunday morning, Rev. Lindsey preached at the Church at Duk Payuel. He could not help making comparison in his own mind to the scene years before. Then, he had felt violently ill, alone and afraid, unprepared. That Church had been brightly lit with sunshine, and he had not known a soul. He had been presented as being a gift, a surprise, the first white clergyman. Now he was known by the Village as a man who had kept his word, who had brought fulfillment of God's promises. Now he was the guest of Pastor Peter. The new Church was a formal Dinka Sanctuary with Chancel platform and pews all hewn out of packed earth, and a tablecloth on the Communion Table. In the congregation were the members of the Medical Mission team.

He read from the Book of Acts, the passage describing the Apostle Paul's Shadow providing healing by falling upon the sick. Rev. Lindsey described that he had come in the shadow of Mother Anon, of John Dau and Paul Ariik, and Jacob Majok. He described the shadow of Don "Majook" Cross, Ted "Mabior" Kinder, Chuck Williams and Mark DeWitt. He described the shadow of the church in Skaneateles that he carried in coming here. He described the shadow of the lives of the people of Duk that had so changed and healed the lives of a people they would never see. He described that healing is not only the technical expertise of medicine, but allowing yourself to be touched by one another, to have your life affected by the caring and faith of others' sacrifices. As he finished and sat down, the Dinka Rector laughed, saying he routinely preached for four hours, but he had heard Americans did not like long sermons.

The Widow's Mite

Like Jesus' story of the widow's mite, a young woman came forward during the offering. While others put shillings, coins and dollars in the basket, she carrying her child, brought a small tub of grain, all her food for the day, to place in the offering to God.

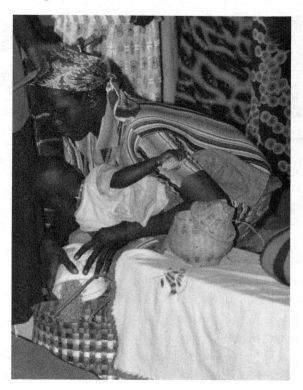

That afternoon the Medical Mission Team began hanging ceiling grids in the Labor/Delivery Room to create a more contained Operating Room. While finding, sorting and washing ceiling materials, the team discovered the adult scale and other tools still boxed in storage rooms covered with debris. Assembling these resources not only improved the capabilities of the clinic, it allowed additional rooms to be put into operation and made the whole facility more hygienic.

At dusk, four men entered the village carrying a blanket. Inside the blanket they carried was a young boy of about nine years of age. Four days prior he had been playing with his father's AK47 rifle, when the gun had gone off. As the boy's wounds were cleaned it became clear the primary trauma was to his right hand, where the ring finger and pinky had been shredded. The boy's left hand had several severe bruises and open sores, there were also several wounds to his chest, to his legs and groin, and to his eye. It appeared the boy had been sitting with the gun braced between his legs, aimed up into the air. He had pulled the trigger with his left hand, while trying to catch the bullet with his right hand. Despite the many additional wounds, those other than his right hand were minor and only needed to be cleaned. The right hand required surgery, as the two fingers had severe compression fractures from the gas of the bullet exploding. The fingers were amputated along the ray between the middle finger and ring finger. The clean wound was left open and allowed to scab, alternating dressings wet to dry. Because the globe of the eye was not pierced, while bruised, the eye will heal. During the examination and surgery, there was no anesthetic and the frightened wounded child whimpered. His father spoke to him once, and the boy quieted all emotions to lay silent.

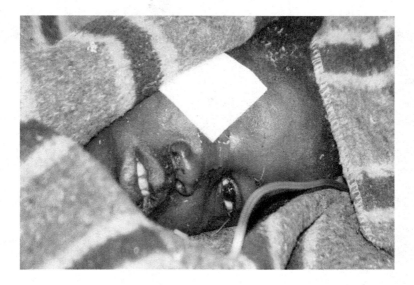

Monday morning was a full day with unanticipated circumstances.

✓ Two men had been in a fight the night before, and in addition to the normal cuts and bruises, one opponent had bitten off the upper lip of the other and swallowed the flesh. Upon examination, because the wound had not exceeded Cupid's bow (the line distinguishing the mucosal skin of the mouth from upper lip flesh) all that needed to be done was to keep the wound clean, and allowed to heal.

✓ Another man had stepped on a thorn which had broken off beneath the skin and become infected. However, the sole of the man's foot was so calloused and thick from walking barefoot all his life, the removal was like pulling a needle through a block of wood.

✓ A child with Cerebral Meningitis was brought in, the child was unable to process and reason, even to follow basic instructions.

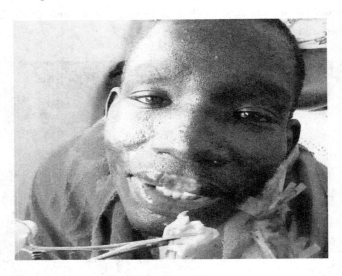

✓ A woman presented with a lymphedema in her back, which caused her extreme pain.

✓ A man described repeated bacterial infections of the penis, requesting circumcision.

✓ A man with Leprosy had lost the end of all his fingers.

✓ A woman had epileptic seizures, seemingly on command, yet she never aspirated, and never wounded herself by her flailing. This was determined to be a psychological matter, as she had reached the age of marriage, and by manifesting seizures she was perceived to be unable to marry.

Shibboleth

✓ Another woman had been captured by the Murle as a young child. She had been unable to speak her native Dinka language and immersed within the Murle culture. She had been raped as she matured, and eventually married to a Murle man, with whom she had three children. After years of mistreatment, one day she learned that the SPLA were near by. She took her infant in her arms and ran for her life.

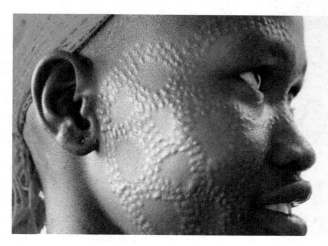

Arriving at the safety of the SPLA with her baby in arm, she now had to prove she was Dinka, yet her skin had been tattooed, her clothing was Murle, her language was Murle, all her customs were Murle. Asked to prove her story, she called up the few Dinka words she recalled from childhood. The stories of King David describe the story of "shibboleth" with deep similarities. The agony of this woman now was that two of her children were still with the Murle, and she desired a means of rescuing them.

Minor surgery was possible under Dr. Geelhoed's close supervision and instruction. For the Medical Mission team members, this presented the dangers and obstacles of performing their very first surgeries, operating in a less than sterile environment. In addition, for many of the Medical Mission team the idea of cutting into a live human being, as well as the sights and smells of surgery made each a little nauseous, though without complication.

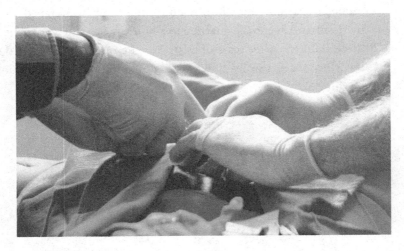

Tuesday presented a series of new and alarming, but related concerns. One man had been given a two-week supply of medication. He reappeared only two days later, claiming he had never been treated and needed medication. When confronted, he admitted to having sold the drugs in the open market, but wanted more medications. At this point the translators became furious with the patient, reprimanding him for having endangered the life of other persons by selling them medications they did not need, and insisted that the patient would not be seen again for two months. Later that morning, a baby was presented with a 3ʳᵈ degree burn on her bottom. The mother described having purchased an ointment that she used for diaper rash, that instead caused the burn.

The Clinic's Dedication: January 10, 2008

On the evening of Wednesday, January 9th, 2008, Dr. Geelhoed and Dr. Lindsey determined they could wait no longer for John Dau's return, they had had no word from John for over a week, so the Clinic Dedication would take place the next day, January 10, 2008. They contacted Pastor Peter, who gathered each of the dignitaries, informing them of the necessity of attending the Clinic Dedication. Rev. Lindsey negotiated with a local man in the marketplace for purchase of a bull for feeding the community at the dedication. Because the team had no large new bills left, Juma, the Clinic Administrator walked to Pok Tap with money from Rev. Lindsey, and traded on the open market for Kenyan Shillings that would be acceptable. A fair price of $300 American dollars was decided for the bull, and Rev. Lindsey gave an additional $50 to the Clinic cooks for their labor and the cost of spices.

Thursday at Noon, the Clinic closed as if for lunch, but instead every one began cleaning up and preparing for the Clinic Dedication. Curiously, the most frequent visitors to the Clinic had been women, as patients or bringing their family members; yet at the Dedication only the male head of households gathered, as this was an official community function. Pastor Peter served as Master of Ceremonies, introducing Rev. Lindsey who described the promise to Supreme Chief Chuiee Deng Leek, description of their first relationship by uniting families separated by war, and that the Clinic was only made possible by joining together the gifts of: Donors, Contractors, the Village, the Presbyterian Church in Skaneateles, and the Clinic staff; he pledged that very soon Satellite Communications would be installed. Rev. Lindsey presented to Pastor Peter a framed plaque with a photo of the First Presbyterian Church in Skaneateles, the 23ʳᵈ Psalm, along with the inscription that the Duk Lost

Boys Clinic had been dedicated this 10th Day of January 2008, by the America Cares for Sudan Foundation.

Dr. Geelhoed spoke next, certifying that as a Medical Doctor licensed by the Sudanese Government in Khartoum he was recognizing the Clinic was of a capacity, and resources to be legitimate as a Primary Health Care Clinic. Dr. Geelhoed too, described that this the Duk Lost Boys Clinic is amazing because people of the Presbyterian Church in Skaneateles, New York, who would never see what they had done, who did not know these people and stood to gain nothing, had given so generously. Then Denise, a Rwandan refugee and applicant to Medical College spoke of what it meant to her as a refugee seeing refugees come home, and John Dau's dream being realized.

The County Commissioner spoke, thanking Rev. Lindsey and Dr. Geelhoed for their work this week, and those who had donated this clinic for their gift. The Local Payam Administrator spoke, describing that he would not presume to say anything different from the County Commissioner, but that he joined in expressing his thanks to Almighty God. After which, John Dau's father, Daniel Deng Leek spoke, then the new Supreme Chief recalling how he had accompanied Rev. Lindsey in choosing the site of the Clinic. Next Elijah the elder, spoke of the history of Sudan and of Duk County. Then a woman spoke, describing that Dinka women rarely speak in public, but she had been asked to do so, because her thumb had been amputated while tying up her cow, and the Clinic had cared for her, and she was alive today because of the clinic.

After which, Juma introduced the Children's Choir from a neighboring village who wished to bless the Dedication with dancing and singing.

As the children finished, a drum beat and wailing began in the distance, as a group of about 50 women of the village danced forward in traditional Dinka dress, singing, telling stories and dancing. Finally, the feast began, as the bull's meat had been roasted and boiled.

The Parable of The Talents

On Friday, the Medical Mission Team completed working at the clinic, and hanging the ceiling in the Labor and delivery rooms. Saturday the plane was set to arrive to return the team to Nairobi. As the first Medical Mission Team waited for the plane to arrive, a woman came up to Rev. Lindsey and looked at him for a long time. She then had a child translate, that he should accompany her. The woman led the way to her hut and had Rev. Lindsey sit upon the ground. She then stared intently into his face, before beginning to dig in the soil. About a foot down, she found a large snail shell, nearly 3" in diameter. She snatched the shell from out of the earth, and wiped it with her shirt, then presented it to the Reverend. Inside the shell was the very $5 bill he had given the woman so many years before. Suddenly, it occurred to him that the parable of the talents had been replayed, as the one he had given $3,000 had created 10 oxen and 5 plows and a program to teach villagers to feed themselves, even passing on the responsibility from one to another. The one who had been given $1,000 had made a business of leasing vehicles that he had charged the clinic for using! And the one who had $5, had buried it in the soil, not judging that God is harsh, but hoping that the stranger would return to fulfill their partnership.

Chaos and Registrations

Days after the first Medical Mission Team returned to the United States, the first email came through, stating that the Satellite Dish and technician had arrived and connected everything for communication. However, the emails also described that the Sudanese who had travelled with John Dau to Uganda for supplies had returned, and there was great turmoil between these Sudanese men and the Kenyan clinic staff. Meeting together as the Board of Directors for America Cares for Sudan Foundation, Dr. David Reed and Dr. Barbara Connor volunteered that they could now travel along with a 3rd year Medical Resident to continue capacity building of the clinic, to restore and create order. David Reed was an Assistant Professor of Emergency Medicine with Academic accreditation to teach at SUNY Upstate Hospital, who was on Sabbatical, going where ever there was need in underdeveloped parts of the world for an Emergency Room Medical Doctor.

Dr. Barbara Connor was able to work at the Clinic for 10 days, then accompany the Medical Director Miriam and Nurse Midwife Cara in leaving, while interviewing Dr. Moses who was being placed at the Duk Lost Boys' Clinic as the new Medical Director by IMA. Dr. Reed and Becky Bollin, the Medical Resident, spent an entire month working at the Clinic. Becky had never been outside the country before, let alone to Sub-Saharan Africa. But having been raised on a Dairy farm with a sister who was a Veterinarian, she proved invaluable as both a Doctor and trusted American professional who knew cattle. Together they began a program of de-worming the entire population of Duk County, as well as seeing patients. One child was brought forward who had a perforation of the uvula, the appendage that hangs down in a person's throat. Not being specialists in this area, the American Medical team took digital photographs and sent these by email to the Syracuse University Hospital, where they were advised against intervention, that the condition could rectify itself naturally. So, demonstrated, was the first experience of tele-medicine at the Duk Lost Boys' Clinic. In future months, a SKYPE account would be created allowing conversation and photos to be shared for free, using the donated Satellite communication service.

Dr. Geelhoed, returned in April with Dr. John Covell of Skaneateles. While this next Medical Mission Team was present, the United Nations High Command for Refugees (UNHCR) relocated 3,000 Dinka additional refugees to Duk Payuel, describing that with a Clinic, sources of water and electricity this village had amenities no other could provide. In addition to working as a Medical Mission Team at the Duk Lost Boys' Clinic, their goal was to make linkages with other clinics, so that cases that might be out of the expertise or medical resources of one might be served by another clinic. One of the Clinics they partnered with is run by Dr. Jill Seeman, an American, who spends eight months of every year working in the oil fields of remote Alaska, as a Medical doctor, to raise enough capital to fund her work at her clinic in Sudan.

Metamorphosis Again into The John Dau Foundation

Recognizing the identification of John Dau's name for Americans, with the film and book God Grew Tired of Us, a new Foundation was created to carry out the work begun by the American Care for Sudan Foundation, this time called the John Dau Foundation. This John Dau Foundation was used as a training ground for Syracuse University students, with the support of continuing members from the American Care for Sudan Foundation. What had begun as a mission of the First Presbyterian Church and had grown into an ecumenical partnership for mission, now going through a metamorphosis into an educational non-profit program with numerous projects. While proselytizing was never part of the American Care for Sudan Foundation, the John Dau Foundation as a university based non-profit program questioned whether to accept "religious-organization" funding.

When Rev. Lindsey had first visited Duk in April 2005, there were 700 residents at Pok Tap and one couple at Duk Payuel. Two years later, there were 1,700 residents at Duk Payuel, which led to the UNHCR relocating 3,000 refugees to this village. Over the next rainy season (eight months), Dinka family members dispersed in countries across Africa came to the same conclusion, totaling 54,000 people in early 2009. One mid-sized church in

Upstate New York acting in mission, had changed the world by building the infrastructure for a village from 2 people to 54,000 residents.

Developing Cold-Chain, Epi, Tb Testing, Counseling and Dots

Numerous Grant Applications were completed, each allowing the Foundation to gain additional registrations and clarify the purpose of projects. Registrations were completed, first for the U.S. Treasury: OFAC (Office of Foreign Assets and Controls) clearance, then DUNS Identification (Registration with Dun & Bradstreet); then CCR (United States Government Central Contractor Registration); then TPIN (Federal Trading Partner Identification Number); then ORC registration with www.//Grants.gov Credential Service Provider; professional investigation by E-Business of Points of Contact (POC); then AOR registration, all in preparation for even being able to submit any grant application. However, until the first formal audit could be completed, there was no track record of financial experience and credibility to demonstrate legitimacy, which finally occurred in early November 2008.

In November 2008, a Trade Union gift of $100,000 allowed the Foundation to have operating income for the next third of a year. Then a gift of $25,000 was received, ear-marked for the creation of a cold-chain. With development of a secure cold-chain, vaccinations would be able to be transported with full efficacy from the pharmaceutical manufacturer, by airplane, to the clinic and distributed to patients, continuously being maintained at given temperature, though the exterior temperature was 120 degrees. In January 2009, the first grant for $450,000 was received as a partner under IRD (International Relief & Development).

In the process of completing US Federal Government registrations, a professional Grant-writer was found, who had a track record and network of contacts for funding NGOs like the John Dau Foundation. This brought yet a new transformation, as the Foundation transitioned from student interns and volunteer Board members also providing service and labor, to contracting for professional services. For the long-term future of the

Foundation and the support of the clinic in Sudan, this transition appeared a practical reality, but not an easily accepted development, as those who had been involved from the beginning were required to give over increasing degrees of control. An ever-present hope for the Foundation had been to turn over all administration to the Clinic staff themselves. The great difficulty is in retraining persons who have lived by responding to the needs of others, that for Western fiscal-responsibility, particularly in receiving grants, there can be no favoritism, no abuses, everything must be objectively and equitably distributed.

Yet an additional element which needed to be balanced and nurtured throughout these years was itinerating and interpreting this mission to others. There were those in the local church who quickly tired of this project; others who questioned the priority of this international project over-against other local missions and denominational causes. Each of those who traveled immediately found themselves so affected by the experience as to become ambassadors, speaking at potluck suppers and pancake breakfasts. The Foundation created a mission sponsorship program, encouraging individuals to pledge $5 or $20 per month every month for a year to three years. These persons were named as "Koiye Miooc" (Koy-ya Mooch) meaning "Generous Persons" in the Dinka language.

In the year 2008 alone, the first year, the Duk Lost Boys' Clinic posted the following statistics:

Superficial Infections - 3,493 cases
      (Hemorrhoids, Herpes Zooster, and Skin Fungal Infections)
Gastrointestinal Abdominal Diseases - 6,047 cases
      (Intestinal Parasites, Gastroenteritis, Peptic Ulcers)
Respiratory Diseases - 5,244 cases
      (Bronchitis, Respiratory Tract Infections and Tuberculosis)
Other Infectious Diseases- 5,994 cases
      (Malaria, Trachoma, Meningitis)
Disorders - 1,485 cases
      (Malnutrition, Anemia, Epilepsy)

Trauma - 715 cases

(Gunshot wounds, burns, scorpion stings)

Maternal/PreNatal Care- 188 Cases

The John Dau Foundation was to use the International Relief and Development (IRD) funds to create an Every Person Inoculation (EPI) Vaccination program, expanding this to create a TB/HIV/AIDS diagnosis/counseling and treatment program, and thereby to develop a Midwife training program. IRD would be able to use the history and experience and name of the Duk Lost Boys' Clinic to create additional clinics in Sudan, the $445,000 being part of a $1.5 million Grant from BSF. IRD assigned large target goals of inoculating 20,000 patients and creating 10 clinics with these funds, all within 18 months, ignoring the timetable that had been necessary to create the first clinic.

Alternative Energy, Hygiene, Public Health, Transportation, Etc

Contractor Don Cross made a commitment to return to Duk in February 2009, arriving three years to the day after he had originally come to Africa, when there had been no clinic and no materials. Cross was able to make structural repairs to the building caused by settling. He then installed a series of solar panels, a wind turbine and batteries to create an alternative power source. This power source was dedicated to a small refrigerator to "create the cold chain" at the clinic. A "dedicated cold-chain" requires that nothing other than medications and lab specimens will ever be kept in this refrigerator; the temperature will be maintained at between 34 and 40 degrees; and that the power source not be compromised by excess electric use for other appliances. Two weeks after Cross' arriving, Drs. Reed and Connor, Don Cross' wife who is a Physician's Assistant, and their daughter who was completing her Master's degree in Public Health arrived at the Clinic, carrying a supply of tetanus vaccinations in a cold chest with dry ice. As the ice chest was opened, having travelled six hours in a small Cessna single engine plane across the Rift Valley and Sahara Desert, at the height of temperatures of the dry season, the temperature inside the chest was 38 degrees, and the consistent temperature of the refrigerator had been verified for three days at 34 degrees, the Cold Chain had been created! Once the population had been vaccinated against tetanus, with a stable refrigerated immunization program, the same processes could be followed for Measles, Mumps, Rubella, Whooping Cough, etc. Reinforcing the Every Person nature of Immunization, 10,000 Anti-malaria impregnated Bed Nets were distributed to every pregnant woman and family with a young child in the area. Like the first Polio vaccination program in America, this required a cultural shift, to believing in and accepting preventative medicine; as well as constantly being vigilant regarding the Black Market, or a belief that if I have one injection was needed for health, multiple injections would be better.

Simultaneously, Dr. Reed worked to teach the Laboratory Technician Peter to create an Acid-fast bucilla testing for verification of Tuberculosis infection cases. Meanwhile, Dr. Connor and Heidi Cross worked with the pharmacist and nurses to create a Direct Observation Treatment System (DOTS) for treatment of Tuberculosis. One of the Sudanese was sent to Nairobi to learn DOTS and HIV/STD counseling. A DOTS program is essential with TB, in that if an individual with Tuberculosis begins treatment, but ceases along the duration, the infection can mutate to become a resistant form of

Tuberculosis, which may be far more highly contagious, and would be unable to be treated. A drug-resistant form of Tuberculosis could easily eliminate an entire population. A DOTS program requires those diagnosed with the disease to return daily, to have a pill placed in their mouth and swallow; and if they do not return, the medical staff seek them out to treat them wherever they are. Once the diagnosis and treatment systems had been created for Tuberculosis, the processes are the same as that for testing HIV/AIDS and other Sexually Transmitted Diseases.

Creation of a Midwifery training program was more difficult, crossing barriers of men being used as Gynecologists, as well as confronting and challenging the anecdotal teaching of homeopathic delivery methods. Yet an experienced Kenyan Midwife trainer was found, who taught 25 Traditional Birthing Attendants a 40-hour class in Birth and Delivery.

Part of the nature of Grant-writing, is modification and adaptation. Originally, Rev. Lindsey had worked with the leadership of IRD to clarify the need and culture for Grant Projects. What routinely occurs, is that Grants are awarded based on a preliminary proposal, then the goals are modified and interpreted based on resources and realities discerned. IRD set several goals which seemed unattainable to the Foundation. However, after the original proposal had been submitted by IRD, a professional grant-writer contacted the Board of Directors of the John Dau Foundation, volunteering her services for a cause she said believed in.

Shortly thereafter she sought her own compensation in order to increase revenues and follow through "on what volunteers could not do." Several of the Board members were concerned, that while she had experience in managing projects in Sudan, her experience had been in Darfur and she had no appreciation for the cultural differences of the Southern, Christian tribes, or their expectations of her as a woman. Among problems encountered were that, IRD had exceptionally high expectations for the numbers that would be effected, without ever having been on site; the grant-writer attempted to make herself indispensable to the grant by not sharing the specific goals required by the grant. Soon after the $445,000 grant was awarded, the grant-writer announced that she would need to go to Sudan to re-hire all the clinic personnel, now as employees of the IRD grant. Her second ultimatum was that while she was in Africa, other Board members should have absolutely no contact with the clinic. While this attempted to create a controlled experience for her to evaluate staff performance, this also created great anxiety and resentment from Board members and Clinic staff. For six weeks, there was no communication between the Board and the Clinic or the Grant-writer (administrator). When she did return, it was to present her letter of resignation. She named the problems of transitioning from a Church-sponsored mission to an on-going International Foundation. She blamed the Clinic staff for what she alleged were abuses, and made these known to other NGOs. She further alienated the IRD staff by challenging IRD's reporting methods and processes. After she left the Foundation, IRD needed to scale down their expectations from creation of 10 Primary Health Care Clinics (PHCC), to equipping of five Primary Health Care Units (PHCU) which are outreach worker staff persons resourcing the Clinic.

Rev. Lindsey then worked with an SU student to complete the United States Government Grant Applicant Certification process, and to apply for United States State Department funding to assist the United Nations in the Jonglei State region of South Sudan. This Grant proposal was for $250,000 to complete all existing projects. The existent air strip barely long enough and wide enough for a single engine Cessna plane to land, would be widened and lengthened for a DC3, allowing the Clinic to have far larger deliveries, thereby decreasing the need for flights to quarterly instead of monthly. Portable solar powered lighting would be made available for the landing strip to allow take-offs and landings after dark. A fence would be installed around the entire Clinic compound for hygiene and safety. In a dowry-culture, cattle wander everywhere dropping feces and tracking this, making germs friable, as well as occasionally the cattle have entered the clinic building. A fence would also permit the patient population one point of entry to the clinic, rather than wandering about the compound. Permanent housing for the staff would provide a sense of permanence and security to the staff, who though they now had tents, had been required to vacate these to sleep in the shipping containers whenever visitors arrived. The solar panels for the dedicated cold-chain had been so successful, the clinic would install 4 kilowatts worth of Alternative Energy power in addition to that for the cold-chain. A second bore-hole water well would be dug, with a new submersible solar powered pump, and storage tank would be installed, allowing the Village to have a clean, available water reservoir whenever needed. A pre-packaged Operating Room of products would be shipped and installed, allowing possibilities of X-ray, and Caesarean sections, Bullet extractions, and other emergency trauma response. An LED Projector would be acquired, to connect to the computer and Internet, allowing possibilities of distance learning.

Two days prior to the Grant Application deadline, the Grant was submitted. Yet, at 2am the following morning an email replied, that the formal registration for Grants.gov was not verified. In the next several days, a flurry of emails and phone calls went back and forth, trying to permit the Application even though the computer system had rejected submission. The USA State Department were extremely helpful and supportive. Finally, this Application was formally denied. However, creating the Grant Application had set the next priority list of projects and cost projections.

December 01, 2009 the Medical Directors performed a site visit to the Clinic, assessing where we now are, and working with staff and volunteers to complete projects. Moses, the Medical Director was discharged for alcohol abuse and insubordination, to be replaced by Leonard Korir who had filled in between Dr. Miriam and Dr. Moses. The following report was submitted on 15 December, 2009.

JOHN DAU FOUNDATION Transforming Health Care in South Sudan

Medical Directors Report to Board of Directors, John Dau Foundation

December 15, 2009

Colleagues,

The medical directors of the Duk Lost Boy's Clinic (Barb Connor, MD and David Reed, MD) have just returned from a site visit to the Duk Lost Boy's Clinic this last week, and in addition had the opportunity to dialog on location over several days with visiting representatives of funding partners BSF and IRD. I am pleased to report substantial progress in many of our foundation and DLBC goals during a period of significant political unrest, and want to share some of these accomplishments as we continue to move forward with the medical objectives of the John Dau Foundation.

In April, 2008, I submitted a report to the board of directors, highlighting what I saw as the most important and immediate short-falls in basic capabilities in our medical operation. Briefly, these included an inability to deliver on what we saw as the highest and most achievable health care priorities:

- Lack of Cold Chain and Immunization program

- Lack of TB/DOTS Capability

- Lack of HIV Testing/Counseling/Treatment program

- Lack of a Dedicated Maternal Health program

- Urgent need for Malaria Education/Net Distribution

- Lack of Emergency Transfusion capability for Maternal Hemorrhage/Trauma

Of note, operation of the clinic without a vehicle has consistently been one of the major logistical handicaps to progress, and today remains one of our greatest needs.

Based on my observations at the clinic over this first week of December, 2009, I can report to you the following accomplishments. These have only been possible through the commitment and leadership from our clinic staff on the ground, generous support from several funding sources, and from a consistent focus of mission throughout the history of the clinic, which since May, 2007, has now delivered care in over 26,000 patient encounters.

✓ Reliable Cold Chain operational since March, 2009; Comprehensive Immunization program is underway and growing rapidly in scope and reach. Of note, inconsistent delivery of vaccines via the GOSS Ministry of Health is now the rate limiting variable in expanding our immunization to the eligible population in the region.

✓ TB/DOTS program has been active since January, 2009. We are capable of diagnosing with laboratory gram stain, and have enrolled ten patients in DOTS, with one treatment failure (patient failing to complete his treatment course).

✓ HIV/AIDS Testing and Treatment: DLBC employee returned from Nairobi Dec 1, 2009. AIDS testing program is now operational, focusing first on pregnant women, and the SPLA military garrison, and are now delivering HIV education and expanding testing to the wider community.

✓ Maternal Health Program: Dedicated Maternal Health clinic has been restored since November, 2009. During first week of December twenty-five active traditional birth attendants from the seven payams of Duk County participated in a 40-hour course in Basic Midwifery, taught by a highly skilled nurse-midwife from Nairobi. This program was uniformly praised by the TBA's and the local leaders, and as a first stage of safe-birth training, will likely have a significant impact in improving child delivery practices in the region. Further training is planned for March, 2010 with these highly motivated traditional birth attendants. Since establishment of the cold-chain, all pregnant women receive a full schedule of tetanus vaccines, treatment for anemia, prophylactic malaria treatment and issued malaria nets. As of December, 2009 they are offered HIV counseling and testing.

✓ Malaria Education and Treatment: Ongoing community health education is taking place on the source and prevention of malaria, throughout our service area, as possible with the limitations of transportation available to us. In March 2009, 1,500 malaria nets were distributed in a focused education and distribution campaign in the two villages closest to the clinic. Last week we were pleased to see nets still prolific and actively used in the community.

✓ Emergency Transfusion Capability: As of December, 2009, emergency transfusion capability has been established, after a focused effort to achieve blood typing, identification of volunteer donors, HIV and Malaria Testing. This capability will likely be lifesaving for patients who have experienced severe post-partum hemorrhage or bleeding from trauma, particularly when civil unrest or inaccessible roads during the wet season prohibit medical evacuation.

Additional developments that will result in enhanced level of medical care:

A Emergency Ultrasound: In November, 2009, Sound *Caring*, the philanthropic arm of Sonosite, Inc, funded Duk Lost Boy's Clinic with a *Titan* Ultrasound at very low cost. This unit will be delivered, with appropriate training, to the clinic by our medical directors in early 2010. This capability will assist in early diagnosis of high risk obstetric patients, facilitating early evacuation of patients with such conditions as breech presentations and placenta previa. It will also serve as a valuable diagnostic aid during management of trauma patients.

4) Computer based reporting of weekly epidemic outbreaks have been submitted to the GOSS Ministry of Health in Juba since March, 2008. The ability to do this via solar-powered satellite internet have positioned Duk Lost Boy's Clinic as the only provider in Duk County that have consistently reported this epidemiologic data, identifying our clinic to GOSS as a capable provider of such outbreak information. Additionally, with cold-chain capability, we serve as a capable facility for response to major epidemics that may occur such as measles, and meningitis. Further, a computerized Excel-based monthly clinic activity report has been standardized that make reporting, trending, and studying local diseases possible to local, state, and GOSS-level agencies, such as the Ministry of Health. These capabilities to measure and report data on regular incident, weekly, and monthly basis, are only possible because of the funding of solar power, satellite internet capability which is not accessible elsewhere in the region.

Examples of routine medical activities that are ongoing, but not the focus of this report, include campaigns for de-worming, Vitamin A supplementation, nutrition assessment, and treatment of infectious diarrhea.

I have, in this report to the board members, attempted to summarize specific accomplishments of the Duk Lost Boys Clinic that have occurred in the last 18 months, and believe that the improvements that have been achieved are the result of <u>deliberate and un-yielding focus</u> to the medical priorities that we have set as a foundation.

We are deeply grateful to our donors, whose generosity has made possible expansion and capacity-building in Duk County. I do look, however, with apprehension, at the unknowns that face the people we serve in terms of political and financial instability, and continue to challenge our organization to stay true to the focus we have to our mission of providing quality health care to the people of our region. We continue to maintain a <u>long-term commitment to provide quality health care</u> to the people of Duk County that will extend beyond specific funding cycles and supporting organizations, and we look forward with hope, to our ultimate goal of completing the transition of the Duk Lost Boy's Clinic to the South Sudanese, as has been the consistent vision of the John Dau Foundation.

Peace Is in Sight

2010, John Dau and Dr. Dave Reed began work with the Moran Eye Hospital in Park City Utah. Following a series of meetings, the staff of Moran agreed to a ten-year commitment to restore eye sight through surgery to 200-300 patients, annually. However, the first two years that Moran attempted to go to South Sudan, they were turned away by violence. The third year, they arrived and surgically restored sight to 300 blind patients over a 2-week site visit! The following year, plans were developed to fly equal number of blind patients from each of the four principal tribes of South Sudan, in order to spend time together in recovery and develop relationships. Health care becoming a "Peace Dividend" was greeted enthusiastically by the people of Duk as well as the Board of the John Dau Foundation. A documentary film by Marmot Films chronicled the eye surgery campaign. This film Duk County like the earlier film God Grew Tired of Us generated excitement at Independent Film Festivals receiving numerous awards.

The Referendum of South Sudan

Departure of the grant-writer/administrator left a void in the administration of the IRD Grant. Tom Dannan had been a Syracuse University student, who upon graduation had served two years in the Peace Corps. Returning to Syracuse, he was seeking employment in something like his Peace Corps experience. Tom sought out each Board Member and listened to their tales of how the clinic had come to be and why. Tom then gave of himself by volunteering to go to Sudan for six months. Tom worked with the Clinic staff to take responsibility and increase their training, while also challenging and working with the BSF Staff to administer the IRD Grant. Infant and Maternal deaths radically decreased. Tom Dannan returned to Central New York in

May, 2010 yet by August was back in Sudan for an additional six months. In 2011, Dan Pisegna replaced Tom as Executive Director continuing commitment.

According to the Peace Accord between North and South Sudan, in January 2011 the people of South Sudan would vote whether to become a separate and independent Nation from the North. The difficulty being that pre-existent conditions cannot continue during the transition; therefore, all Non-Governmental Organization (NGO) grants had to end December 31, 2011. As the first grant concluded, the Foundation applied for a renewal to carry the clinic through December 2011. However, to promote indigenous development, the renewal grant provided nothing for transportation. While a noble concept, a blanket denial of all transportation of goods and services ignored how remote the clinic is and the difficulty of transportation during the rainy season.

Envisioning the future, John Dau described (July 2010) "One of three things will happen. The Referendum will take place peacefully and successfully the Nation of Sudan will divide allowing self-rule. If so the clinic will continue to develop and become part of the infra-structure of the new society. Or the Northern Government will disrupt the elections, seize the results, in some way negate the validation. If so, for several weeks after the referendum there will be peace as people decide what to do, then there will be war again. Or the referendum will occur, but one of the SPLA Generals will be displeased with his power in the new Government and he will begin a war of his own. In either of these last situations, we would need to evacuate our people and the clinic would need to close." Don Cross speculated that if the clinic were to close, anything of value, the Solar Panels and electrical circuitry, the Satellite Dish, Medical equipment and tools would all be scavenged. Dr. David Reed volunteered, "I am not certain what the clinic staff would do. Most are now from Duk, this is their home. Possibly the clinic would stay open as a place of refuge and medicine in response to war." Others responded whether the clinic being a large metallic building with Satellite Dish in the middle of a wilderness might not prove a great target. Rev. Lindsey spoke to John Dau in front of the Board of Directors. "Remember when I first went to Sudan alone. Chuiee Deng Leek, your uncle, the Supreme Chief of all the Dinka offered a blessing and curse, saying "You have offered a great thing in reuniting our people with our sons and daughters, and in pledging to provide a hospital. If you do as you have said, you will be blessed, living a long and full life; but many have lied to us and not followed their words. If you have lied, you will die a miserable and painful death." Do you remember this, as I do? Then please carry this word back to Chuie Deng Leek, "We have done what we have pledged, and because of this not a single child or mother has died in delivery. Your people are growing strong and healthy because of the care provided through this clinic. Now it is up to you to follow through. If you allow the clinic to be destroyed, and the staff to be threatened, health care will end and your people will again be a suffering people dying miserable and painful deaths. But if you have faith and follow through in development of this project and this new Nation, then your people and your Nation will be blessed."

September 2012 the JDF Board held a Fund-Raising Celebration. One of the highlights of the event was Video Conference with Paramount Chief Chuie Deng Leek confirming the Blessing, that Pregnant Mothers and little children all know your name and sing praises of the Skaneateles Presbyterian Church.

The Struggles of a New Nation

Today, we look nostalgically at the period of Nation-building in the United States of America following the Revolution. But try to imagine, if that fragile period of declaring our freedom as a Nation had also been America's Civil Rights Era of the 1960s, confronting whether all persons of every ethnic group and tribe are equal. Eighteen months after celebration of the referendum of South Sudan, the fragile new Nation of South Sudan was ripped asunder, as the President and Vice President of South Sudan each attempted to have the other killed, because the President was of the Dinka tribe and the Vice President was of the Nuer tribe.

February 28, 2014 the Lost Boys Clinic at Duk Payuel was looted by 3000 Soldiers. The Solar Panels were removed and sold. All of the doors and windows of the clinic were broken. All of the contents of the Clinic compound were stolen or destroyed. Due to forethought, the Solar powered Ultra-Sound Machine, and a new Ambulance were hidden in safety in Juba and all the staff were scattered to other villages. When the rebel soldiers arrived, Paramount Chief James Chuie Deng Leek placed himself between the Clinic building and the troops. Even a Paramount Chief is only a man, and Chuie Deng Leek was kidnapped by 17 of the young rebels. However, the buildings themselves could not be destroyed. The following day, Paramount Chief Chuie Deng Leek escaped unharmed. Despite other Villages and cities being leveled in these same riots, the Clinic buildings at Duk Payuel still stood.

While all work was temporarily suspended due to insecurity, the reality was that a decade prior there had been no clinic. Prior to 2006 there had been no staff, as the general population did not have any education beyond the 3rd Grade. The nearest medical care had been 75 miles away and there were no roads. There had been no clinic, and expectations were that when you became ill, you died. At this point in 2013, despite violence, fear and insecurity, the Clinic Buildings remain, the Clinic staff still have their skills and program experience, and are anxious to return to work. The funding source described that due to the devastation, if any health care can be provided at the clinic, all dollars will be available for rebuilding, regardless of program successes and deliver-ables. So while, the worst possible devastation was endured, in the end, the Clinic buildings and compound, the staff and funding, and the population's expectations remain strong. In July 2014, it was reported that 1,000 patients per week were being treated by the Medical Staff, and that in the month of July alone over 9,000 new patients were inoculated against diseases (Polio, Measles, Vitamin A Deficiency, Albendazole), all without the Clinic facilities.

The tribal violence and presence of rebel soldiers had prevented any food from being planted. The ground was burned. In village upon village, every building was leveled. This devastation created one of the worst conditions of famine in modern history. Adding insult to injury, the famine came at the same time as international news of an Ebola Virus spreading across West

Africa. News cycles being what they are, all reference to famine was lost in the Western World, as the Center for Disease Control released reports of persons in Liberia dying from a mysterious virus that presented like the flu or common cold. Grant funding for Maternal/Child health care was suspended; however new grants were made available for combatting malnutrition. The JDF staff mobilized around three UNICEF grants providing food to Severely Acute Malnourished (SAM) children under 5 years of age.

In the year 2015, with no Building, the Duk Lost Boys' Clinic posted the following statistics:

Affliction	Number of Cases	Specifics
Superficial Infections	1,100 cases	(Hemorrhoids, Herpes Zooster, Skin Fungal Infections)
Gastrointestinal Disease	458 cases	(Intestinal Parasites, gastroenteritis, Peptic Ulcers)
Respiratory Diseases	1,000 cases	(Bronchitis, Respiratory Tract Infections, Tuberculosis)
Other Infectious Disease	6,028 cases	(Malaria, Trachoma, Meningitis)
Others Disorders	6,053 cases	(Malnutrition, Anemia, Epilepsy)
Trauma	167 cases	(Gunshot wounds, burns, scorpion stings)
Maternal/PreNatal Care	32,867 cases	
Total Patient Consults	180,335 cases	

As armistice has again been created, the Clinic is in start-up, while staff attempt to reclaim the building and compound from encroaching wilderness. However, the Clinic is now located in a Nuer Tribal region. In addition to Tribal anxiety and animosity, the reality is that the Dinka and Nuer people do not speak the same language, so new staff will need to be recruited for the Clinic who speak Nuer. By being forced outside our Clinic compound, JDF discovered 20,000 people living on 47 islands located in the Nile Rivers, a severely malnourished population who have never before been medically served.

TRANSITIONS TO EMERGENCY NUTRITION SERVICES

During this period, JDF shifted priority to Emergency Nutrition Services. OFDA reported services of JDF in the following report.

In September of 2014, the security situation permitted JDF to once again resume operations in Poktap, Duk County. With assistance from OFDA, a nutrition programming was reinstated in Duk County. By December 2014 Nutritional programs were in full swing and JDF had established a base for nutrition operations in Poktap. This location was being developed into a PHCU which would be the base of nutrition operations for JDF in Duk County. By January 2015, JDF expanded nutrition programs into more remote regions of Duk County in order to conduct additional screenings and feeding for SAM/MAM (SAM=Severe Acute Malnutrition / MAM=Moderate Acute Malnutrition). By March of 2015, JDF had reached the north of Duk County and permanently placed a fixed site screening and feeding location in Ayueldit. Due to the movement of Internally Displaced Persons (Refugees) in Duk County, the Ayueldit base of operation was moved to Padiet in March of 2016. Ayueldit is still an active JDF mobile nutrition site.

ACF partial SMART assessment findings:

An independent survey conducted in Poktap in January of 2016, assessed a total of 475 children aged 6-59 months (230 Boys/ 245 Girls), from 420 households. Nutritional and morbidity status were measured of these children.

The results of this assessment found that the malnutrition rate in Poktap is classified as Critical in accordance with WHO classification, in that GAM (Global Acute Malnutrition = the combination score for MAM and SAM) was exceeding the 15% Emergency Threshold. In addition, Poktap results indicated high prevalence of diseases with 61.9% of the children having had an episode of illness two weeks prior to the survey. Main illnesses reported were fever, cough, and diarrhea. These illnesses were attributed primarily to seasonal swamps and stagnant waters in the area, and poor WASH (Basic Hygiene) practices including open defecation. The increase in rate of malnutrition was primarily attributed to the increase of new Households arriving to Poktap daily. These new arrivals were more likely to be suffering from malnutrition as they were primarily coming from areas where no nutrition services were previously available.

Key recommendations from the Nutrition Survey include continuing to strengthen Nutrition services and scaling up services where possible. The intent was to provide more comprehensive access to treatment for Duk County residents. Recommendations included taking measures to strengthen community screening activities for early detection of SAM cases; increasing resources to allow mobile teams the ability to reach the areas where access if difficult; and increased education.

Inter-Agency Rapid Assessment of Duk County:

By January of 2016, the nutrition cluster and partners heard of the rapidly growing population in Duk County and decided to conduct an assessment to confirm new arrivals to the county, and additional needs. The interagency survey conducted from February 8th 2016 through February 12th 2016 confirmed that populations of IDPs and returnees to Duk County were rising rapidly. As many as 30 new households / a day were currently arriving in Duk County. Many of the new arrivals were traveling to Duk in search of food and other humanitarian assistance. The report also found that a significant portion of the children arriving in Duk were orphaned. Although the sample size of this survey was relatively small, and therefore may not represent the entire population, the assessment found that SAM in the county Prevalent, especially among new arrivals. Of the 228 children and 56 PLW (Pregnant or Lactating Women) from 4 villages screened, 20.6% (47) were found to be SAM; 24.1% (55) were MAM; and 26.8% (61) were at risk of developing malnutrition. The GAM rates recorded were very high 46.7 % (SAM=20.6% and MAM= 24.1%) with 1.3% Oedema cases observed. 28.6% of the assessed children were found to be at risk of developing malnutrition (12.5cms- 13.5cms) this shows an impending nutrition crisis. Only 28.5% (65) of the surveyed children were well nourished and out of danger of developing malnutrition. The nutrition situation of Pregnant or Lactating Women (PLW) was also found to be alarming. Of all the PLW measured 16.1% (9) were severely malnourished with measurement of the circumference of their upper arm less than 21cms; and 53.6% (30) moderate malnourished with circumference of upper arms between 21-23cms. Only 30.4% (17) were well nourished > 23cms.

In Ayueldit, out of 48 children screened, it was found that 7 (14.6%) were SAM.

In Padiet, from 80 children screened, 28 (35%) were identified as SAM.

In Panjak, from 72 children under 5years old screened, 9 (12.5%) were SAM, and

In Poktap (where JDF was established and had been operational for 1 year), from 28 Under 5 year olds screened, 0 (0%) were identified as SAM. These results showed an alarming nutrition situation, which needs an urgent intervention to save the community from death due to malnutrition.

Nutrition cluster recommendations included moving JDF static nutrition location from Ayueldit across the canal to Padiet (about 3 KM away). Padiet was the fastest growing village in the county with most new arrivals settling in this area. Padiet also had the highest rates of GAM in the county. The nutrition cluster also recommended that JDF develop this site into a Malnutrition Site in order to better cope with complex nutrition cases. JDF was given a location in Padiet by the community, and in February of 2016, moved from Ayueldit to Padiet. With assistances, JDF began putting in place the infrastructure to develop this site. This site is now fully functional, but additional resources are needed.

JDF Activities and OFDA Priorities:

The JDF Emergency Nutrition Response Program directly address Nutrition issues in Duk County by extending services to conflict affected populations residing in Duk County. JDF is currently managing 2 Sites in Poktap and Padiet. JDF recently established a third static site in Duk Payuel and a forth Static site in Koyoom islands. The Koyoom Islands represents the largest gap in nutrition services in Duk County, mainly due to the inaccessibility of the location. No organization has ever conducted health or nutrition services of any kind in Koyoom islands because it was thought to be too difficult. JDF was the first Non-Governmental Organization to operate there and our nutrition site is now up, functional, and saving lives.

Overall, the JDF/OFDA emergency nutrition project has been extremely successful, actual results far exceeding expected results. This is in part due the increase of population size of Duk County during the program period. The project was originally designed for an estimated population of 68,000. The population of Duk County grew to an estimated 100,000 to 110,000 during the project. This population increase threatened to overwhelm the project. But with the assistance from the nutrition cluster and OFDA (USA Office of Foreign Disaster Assistance), and in-kind support form UNICEF / WFP (World Food Program), JDF was able to develop the program to cope with the growing population. Increases in patient population, meant JDF easily achieved performance markers for this project. JDF recommendations for the improvement of the program design include additional on-site training for nutrition staff. JDF nutrition staff have experience in implementing and managing nutrition programs; however, refresher training by nutrition experts would benefit the program highly. JDF recommends that OFDA nutrition programs provide a multi-day on site nutrition training for staff, quarterly.

Additional recommendations include project continuity. The recent emergency nutrition response program which ended May 31st 2016 was highly successful. However, the need is still present. In fact, the need in Duk County has grown since the start of the project as IDPs came to Duk in order to have access to the Nutrition programs. Unfortunately, there is a funding gap in the county because of lack of continuity which threatens to undo all the work JDF has done over the last 14 months.

Beneficiaries:

Below is a complete list of beneficiaries targeted during this project. The table below represents estimated population figures as of April 2015 when this project began. In January 2016, a large influx of returnees and refugees (IDPs= Internally Displaced Persons) hit Duk County. Many new arrivals chose to settle around the north of Duk County in the Padiet area, and in the east of Duk County around the Payuel area. Exact population of Duk at this time is not known, but the current population of Duk is thought to be between 100,000 and 110,000. Populations coming to Duk and settling in the north are primarily IDPs from Ayod and Uror coming to access nutrition, medical, and other services. Populations settling in the South (Poktap region) and East (Payuel region) are primarily returnees seeking to resettle Duk County. Many returnees are settling near Payuel because of ease of access to World Food Program distribution sites. Upon review of the screening data, it is possible to see a slight increase in the prevalence of SAM/MAM from January through May 2016. This is due to the increase of new arrivals to Duk County who are more likely to present as SAM/MAM.

Beneficiaries by Population and Location in Duk County:

Location	Total	Pop	Site Type
Poktap	Ageer Payam	16307	Fixed Site

Comments: Operation Base: Community mobilization, screening, micronutrient supplement, deworming, health & nutrition education.

Duk Payuel	(Duk Payuel Payam)	5000	Fixed Site

Comments: This is the site of the Duk Lost Boys Hospital. It is also the site of the WFP Rubb Hall so a central distribution point for Duk. Community mobilization, screening, micronutrient supplementation, deworming, health and nutrition education.

Patuenoi	(Duk Apyuel Payam)	Mobile Outreach site	Accessible from Payuel
Pajut	(Panyang Payam)	Mobile Outreach site	Accessible from Payuel.

This site requires a static location; however, insecurity prevents establishment at this time.

Padiet		31247	Fixed Site

Base of Operations for all locations in N. Duk County. This region of Duk is growing rapidly, actual population is much higher, exact number not known Community mobilization, screening, micronutrient supplementation, deworming, health & nutrition education.

Panajak	Dorok Payam	Mobile Outreach Site A	ccessible from Padiet
Buongjok	Dorok Payam	Mobile Outreach Site	Accessible from Padiet
Amiel	Dongchak Payam	Mobile Outreach Site	Accessible from Padiet
Dorok	Dorok Payam	Mobile Outreach Site	Accessible from Padiet
Ayueldit	Dongchak Payam	Mobile Outreach Site	Accessible from Padiet
Ayankou	Padiet Payam	Mobile Outreach Site	Accessible from Padiet
Panyanbil	Dongchak Payam	Mobile Outreach Site	Accessible from Padiet
Koyoom	Dongchak Payam	15500	New Fixed Site Facility

This site was established in May 2016 as base of operation reaching 47 inhabited islands.

JDF is the only NGO to operate, Nutrition, WASH, and Health services of any kind in this location. Sites below are islands with major populations. Community mobilization and screening, micronutrient supplementation, deworming, health and nutrition education.

Kaweer	Dongchak Payam	Mobile Outreach Site	Accessible from Koyoom
Malua	Dongchak Payam	Mobile Outreach Site	Accessible from Koyoom
Moldova	Dongchak Payam	Mobile Outreach Site	Accessible from Koyoom
Mayen	Dongchak Payam	Mobile Outreach Site	Accessible from Koyoom
Watkuach	Dongchak Payam	Mobile Outreach Site	Accessible from Koyoom
Atueke	Dongchak Payam	Mobile Outreach Site	Accessible from Koyoom
Loong	Dongchak Payam	Mobile Outreach Site	Accessible from Koyoom
Fly Camp	Dongchak Payam	Mobile Outreach Site	Accessible from Koyoom
Ciranmaar	Dongchak Payam	Mobile Outreach Site	Accessible from Koyoom
Panom-athanduk	Dongchak Payam	Mobile Outreach Site	Accessible from Koyoom
Angot	Dongchak Payam	Mobile Outreach Site	Accessible from Koyoom
Wanteny	Dongchak Payam	Mobile Outreach Site	Accessible from Koyoom

Total in Koyoom Islands   68,045

The data below was collected at JDF static and mobile nutrition points throughout Duk County. Surveillance data used to measure results was routine data collected on site by JDF data managers. This data reflects number SAM/MAM patients identified each month during monthly mass screenings at JDF static and mobile nutrition locations. The data below is a snapshot of the community, which can be used to calculate rates of SAM/GAM. This data does not necessarily reflect new admissions, nor does it include existing nutrition patients coming to JDF clinic sites for weekly rations. Patients who were identified as SAM/MAM during routine screenings, and who were not existing patients were referred to the JDF clinics for admission, or were admitted on site.

Duk County Screening Data: April 2015- May 2016

Duk County U5 Nutrition Data	Apr	May	Jun	Jul	Aug	Sep	Oct
Duk County U5 Nutrition Data	2631	1210	2724	2349	2578	1851	1852
Girls 6-59 Months Screened	2083	1644	2218	2262	2135	1714	1856
Total 6-59 months	4714	2854	4942	4611	4713	3565	3708
Total SAM Identified	75	114	92	86	70	48	63
Total MAM Identified	373	282	254	289	292	189	172
Percentage of GAM	9.5%	10.37%	7%	3.79%	5.55%	6.65%	6.64%
Percentage of SAM	1.59%	3.99%	7%	1.86%	1.48%	1.34%	1.7%

Duk County Under 5 Nutrition Data	Nov	Dec	Jan	Feb	Mar	Apr	May
Boys 6-59 Months Screened	1314	1645	2372	2563	1936	1058	1778
Girls 6-59 Months Screened	1338	1404	2406	2648	1646	1242	2031
Total 6-59 months	2652	3049	4778	5211	3582	2300	3809
Total SAM Identified during Screening	72	67	72	108	102	160	163
Total MAM Identified during Screening	197	199	235	186	215	253	266
Percentage of GAM	10.14	8.72	6.43	5.64	8.85	17.95	11.26
Percentage of SAM	2.71%	2.19%	1.5%	2.07%	2.84%	6.95%	4.28%

	Total
Boys 6-59 Months Screened	27861
Girls 6-59 Months Screened	26627
Total 6-59 Months Screened	54488
Total SAM Identified during Screening	1292
Total MAM Identified during Screening	3402
Percentage of GAM	8.61
Percentage of SAM	2.37

(PLW=Pregnant or Lactating Women)

	Apr	May	Jun	Jul	Aug	Sep	Oct
PLW Screened	1540	527	1091	212	865	644	727
PLW SAM Admitted	26	38	25	11	14	14	18
Percentage of PLW SAM	1.69%	7.21%	3.19%	5.19%	1.62%	2.79%	2.17%

	Nov	Dec	Jan	Feb	Mar	Apr	May	Total
PLW Screened	302	703	714	860	826	327	352	9690
PLW SAM Admitted	11	9	15	23	11	17	243	
Percentage of SAM PLW	3.64%	1.28%	2.09%	2.67%	1.33%	3.36%	4.8%	2.5%

Goals and Accomplishments

JDF far exceeded all program targets during the project period. As demonstrated in the figures below, this program saved lives. As previously mentioned, one reason the targets were achieved so easily is because the increase in the patient population within Duk substantially increased the number of patients presenting with SAM/ MAM, and increased the need. Although this increase in population threatened to overwhelm the program, JDF (with the help of nutrition cluster partners) developed additional infrastructure at existing nutrition sites, and established new nutrition lactation, to cope with the growing need. With partner support, we managed to do this on or under budget in all categories (with the exception of management). Although this program was extremely successful, additional support is still needed to maintain and continue the work JDF has started.

Constraints

During the program period, JDF was able to overcome numerous constraints. Major difficulties included, Logistical support and supply chain, as well as coping with the increasing number of SAM/MAM cases due to increasing IDPs residing in Duk County. With the support from partners and the logistics cluster, JDF overcame supply chain issues by airlifting in nutrition goods when necessary. WFP did two airdrops which resupplied nutrition facilities during the wet season. During the wet season, wet roads prevented JDF from conducting outreach to certain locations. To overcome this barrier, JDF staff would at times walk up to 10 miles carrying plumpy-nut on their heads. The dedicated staff of JDF often make this sacrifice in order to make sure SAM children do not die.

Increasing patient population in Duk County also presented a significant constraint during the program period. JDF appealed to the nutrition cluster for assistance and they responded. JDF was lucky to partner with ACF (Action Contre La Faim). ACF nutrition professionals lived and trained JDF staff on site from February to May 2016. They also provided in-kind support and helped JDF develop Padiet. With this support, JDF was able to provide quality comprehensive care to a growing Duk County Patient population.

JDFOFDA Emergency Nutrition Response Program Indicators

No.	Sub-sector	Indicator Baseline	OFDA Targets	Actual Achieved	% of Objective
1	Infant /Young Child	Exclusive breast 0-6 months	794	4601	580%
2	6 mo.< 24 mo.	Daily food in 4 food groups	2383	9580	402%
3	Behavior Change Interventions		16552	20326	123%
4	Management of MAM Number MAM Sites		7	4 Static/ 5 Mobile	129%
5	Number Admitted to MAM (New Cases)		1442	2806	195%
6	Number trained in MAM		20	58	290%
7	Management of SAM Number trained in SAM		20	66	330%
8	Number of OPT and SC sites		2 SC	2 Static OTP / 5 Mobile OTP	129%
9	Number treated for SAM (New Cases)		1019	1435	141%
10	Number Completing SAM		734	852	116%
11	Nutrition Systems, guidelines, protocols		20	54	320%
12	Number of reports received on time		12	14	117%
13	Number of stock outs		10	6	60%

Cost Analysis

JDF came in or under budget in all aspects of the program except management. This was due to in-kind support from UNICEF, WFP, ACF. In addition to logistical support from the logistics cluster. Management was slightly over budget. This is due to the increase in the patient population within Duk County which required additional management capacity. The cost overrun in management was not significant as it was under 10% of the management budget.

Exchange rate fluctuations were not a significant factor as JDF budgets and pays staff in USD.

Conclusion

No one can explain the grace of God: why these refugees, came to this Church, at this time, in either one's life. The Church did learn to have a Bible close at hand, and to use the Word of God. The Church developed new relationships with one another, because of new relationships with God and with these refugees, the Church learned to respond to the Call of God. In all these ways, this Church became a servant people, responsive to the needs of others, rather than a programmatic Church, or a survivor or pillar Church.

Rev. Lindsey created a new paradigm for doing mission. Projects begin under the supervision of the Mission Committee of the Session, with administrative costs and administrative support managed by the Church. But when the mission is a stable partner, the Church Session would intentionally "birth" the mission as an independent, non-profit corporation with its own Board of Directors, Budget, and Tax Identification Status. In this way, encouraging expansion of the mission beyond what could be done as an on-going Church program, as a true mission partnership with the Church while giving up all control. Being a servant people, this Church now is responsive and attentive to the need for prayer, and have witnessed prayer working miracles. Medical students learned they did not have to have MRIs and CAT Scans to provide medicine. American understandings of money were re-interpreted, as a people who had given far more than they imagined possible in building campaigns, then found resources to provide health care and build a Clinic on the opposite side of the world. There was nothing linear and logical in how this mission developed. A partnership of trust and mission commitment was forged. According to the principles of forging steel, there is extreme heat, and pressure and a life jarring pounding, as disparate elements become one. At the same time, a people with no community development, a stone-aged oppressed people, partnered with people in America as trusted friends. This people received quality health care.

The idea of covenant is as ancient as Abraham, Noah, Eve and Adam. Part of Post-Modernism is a reactionary responsiveness rather than a planned and calculated rationalism. A questioning of how shall we react to each given circumstance, responding to presenting issues without full understanding of long-range impacts. One of the lessons learned in this experience has been the depth of willingness needed to react and respond in order to fulfill the covenant, no matter the circumstance. Opportunities have been presented throughout these years, at times by adversity, at which point the faith question became, will you give up, or will you reach out again and try? The question of the County Commissioner in 2005 had been, "We have responsibility to name our needs. You must decide if you can accept the covenant to partner with us or not." In essence this is the Old Testament question of Covenant, the question of the Cross, and trust in God's grace.

This experience of mission in Sudan has demonstrated a different paradigm for a Church of North American Protestants, to live into covenant, uncertain where we are going, if we are going in the right direction, except to hope we are in partnership with God and relationship with one another. The poem "The Road Less Traveled", emphasizes that the choices we take make all the difference. There have been numerous occasions in this mission partnership where a dead-end was encountered. Occasions when God reached out, in a new Calling, in response to death. Every time, at every ending/death, someone was inspired to step forward to respond to the Call. Too easily in 20th Century North America, people have given up. Marriage was difficult, requiring compromise and change; business changed, the economy or

141

technology shifted. Partnership with God requires a covenant commitment cut into our hearts, into the body of Christ, into our very own flesh and lives, that we will continue and try to respond faithfully to the Call of God.

Bibliography of Citations:

Dau, John Bul, *God Grew Tired Of Us: A Memoir,* National Geographic, Washington, DC, 2007.

Leas, Speed, *Discover Your Conflict Management Style,* Alban Institute, Bethesda, MD., 1997.

About the Author

The Rev. Dr. Craig Lindsey is Pastor of The First Presbyterian Church of Skaneateles, New York, USA. A graduate of the College of Wooster, Ohio in Urban Planning and Community Development; Union Theological Seminary in the City of New York, NY; and Columbia Theological Seminary in Decatur, Georgia with his Doctor of Ministry in The Gospel in A Postmodern Culture, his thesis work on *Essentials Necessary for Congregational Redevelopment: Restoring Salt's Savor*. Rev. Lindsey is a member of the Sudan Mission network of the Presbyterian Church USA. He is also one of the Founding members of the Board of Directors and Secretary of the John Dau Foundation. Rev. Lindsey is married to Judy, and they are the parents of C. Michael who lives and works in Brooklyn, NY; and Nathan who is completing his PhD at UC Berkeley CA in the field of Magneto-tellurics.

CPSIA information can be obtained
at www.ICGtesting.com
Printed in the USA
FSOW04n0559131216
28505FS